Barb & Wilma,

From our home to yours. Our door is always open ~ when you're looking for the Prairies, our front and back doors open to the pages of this book.

Thank you for the wonderful hospitality!

Lois

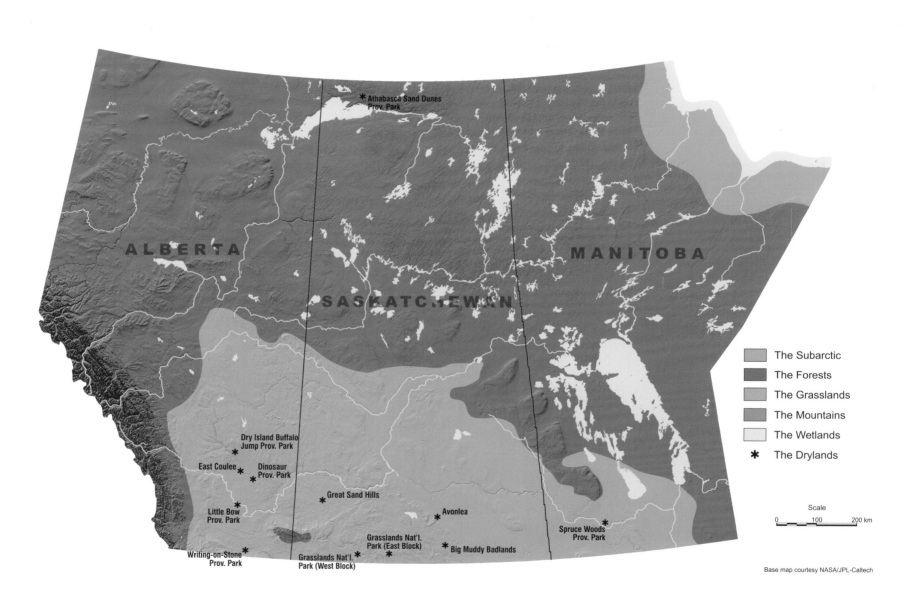

* Athabasca Sand Dunes
  Prov. Park

ALBERTA

MANITOBA

SASKATCHEWAN

The Subarctic

The Forests

The Grasslands

The Mountains

The Wetlands

* The Drylands

Dry Island Buffalo
Jump Prov. Park

East Coulee *

Dinosaur
Prov. Park

Little Bow
Prov. Park

* Great Sand Hills

* Avonlea

Spruce Woods
Prov. Park *

Grasslands Nat'l.
Park (East Block)

Writing-on-Stone
Prov. Park

Grasslands Nat'l.
Park (West Block)

* Big Muddy Badlands

Scale

0   100   200 km

Base map courtesy NASA/JPL-Caltech

OVERLEAF: *Stones and grasses*
GRASSLANDS NATIONAL PARK, SK

Mike Grandmaison's

Prairie

and beyond

Photographs by Mike Grandmaison | Text by Jan Volney

TURNSTONE PRESS

I dedicate this book to my "prairie family"—my wife Annette,
my daughters Nadine and Vanessa, my son-in-law Colin, my grandson Riley,
my granddaughter Summer, and my father-in-law Barry.

Mike Grandmaison's Prairie and Beyond
Copyright © Mike Grandmaison 2012

Turnstone Press
Artspace Building, 206-100 Arthur Street
Winnipeg, MB R3B 1H3 Canada
www.TurnstonePress.com

Turnstone Press gratefully acknowledges the assistance of the Canada Council for the Arts, the Manitoba Arts Council, the Government of Canada through the Canada Book Fund, and the Province of Manitoba through the Book Publishing Tax Credit and the Book Publisher Marketing Assistance Program.

Cover and Interior Design: Jamis Paulson | Map: Weldon Hiebert | Text: Jan Volney | Photographs: Mike Grandmaison, www.grandmaison.mb.ca
Fine art photographs available through www.thecanadiangallery.com
Printed and bound in Canada by Friesens for Turnstone Press.

Library and Archives Canada Cataloguing in Publication

Grandmaison, Mike, 1954-
    Mike Grandmaison's prairie and beyond / Mike Grandmaison (photographer) ; Jan Volney (text).

ISBN 978-0-88801-393-4

    1. Landscape photography--Prairie Provinces. 2. Nature photography--Prairie Provinces. 3. Prairie Provinces-Pictorial works.
4. Natural history--Prairie Provinces--Pictorial works.

I. Volney, Winston Jan Anthony, 1946- II. Title.

FC3237.G72 2012   971.20022'2   C2012-901277-7

Contents

Introduction

The word 'prairie' often evokes a vision of flat, endless, and uninteresting landscapes. However, those who live on the prairie, who know the land intimately, understand that there is so much more to the region than this inaccurate preconception. While I was not born on the prairie, it has surrounded me for the past thirty years. I can no longer imagine my home anywhere else.

In the late seventies I left Sudbury, looking for work as a biologist in Edmonton. Coming from a land of rock, water, and trees in north central Ontario, the prairie revealed itself quite dramatically as my train travelled off the Precambrian Shield and onto the plains. For the next few days I was fastened to the dome car window in awe of the captivating landscape that would become my new home. While I expected the view to be 'as flat as a pancake,' the path I travelled proved to be remarkably diverse. Farm fields lined with shelter belts gave way to rolling hills dotted with potholes. One minute there was a prairie slough, the next, what appeared to be arid and desert-like habitat. This place was remarkable. I came to understand that the Prairie provinces consisted of much more than just wheat fields, cow pastures and abandoned homesteads. There was texture and character here. I instantly fell in love.

I was fortunate during my years in Alberta to travel the length and breadth of the province, and through my work spent time in Saskatchewan, Manitoba, British Columbia, and the Northwest Territories. As a budding photographer, I was more than fortunate to have access to innumerable

OPPOSITE: View of the Bolton Farm and home of the Rayner family
BALJENNIE, SK

subjects and environments. I honed my skills whenever given an opportunity, spending countless hours on weekends travelling the back roads in search of new subject matter. Seeing the majestic Canadian Rockies for the first time was an unforgettable experience, leaving me with a sense of awe and wonder from the beauty and grandeur of such a remarkable landmark. Being able to capture the alpine glow above the mountain peaks around Herbert Lake and seeing an early snowfall completely envelop a blazing autumn scene in Waterton Lakes National Park changed the way I looked at the changing of the seasons. Descending into the eerie badlands of Dinosaur Provincial Park was no less memorable. The quiet beauty of Saskatchewan, its legendary 'living skies' over endless fields of wheat, barley, and canola resonate within me today. Truly, I learned my craft on the prairie.

In the mid eighties, I transferred to Winnipeg, almost at the other end of the prairies I knew. Here, I explored countless lakes and rivers in the Precambrian Shield. The rock reminded me of picking blueberries with my dad on the knoll behind the family cottage. The place definitely felt like home, but quite different. Along with the varied, colourful agricultural zone, the unusual Carberry Desert, the endangered tall grass prairie near Tolstoi, and the subarctic region of the Hudson Bay Lowlands charmed me. Near Churchill, I saw the powerful polar bear which is now, unfortunately, a species at risk. Manitoba, it seemed, was equally as mysterious and serendipitous a place as Alberta. Some ecological regions, or biomes, were similar, though distributed differently, but the treasure their landscapes held for me were immense.

Over the past fifteen years, I have contributed to various book projects, many in Ontario. However, I have always wanted to publish a book about my adopted home. With *Prairie and Beyond*, I can finally showcase my appreciation for the region. The 'prairies' for the purposes of this book are defined as the provinces of Manitoba, Saskatchewan, and Alberta. Their landscape goes far beyond the grasslands to include a variety of habitats, and because these habitats are not contained within political borders and are shared throughout the area, I divided the book into chapters based on the broad biomes found within the prairie region, rather than into individual provinces. In addition to grasslands and agricultural lands, the prairie region also features deserts, badlands, mountains, and tundra, along with forests and wetlands. This loose classification of the region by habitat, as shown in the map at the front of the book, is the basis for organizing the various photographs.

Selecting the images for this book proved to be quite challenging, particularly for the grasslands chapter. As you can well imagine, I have spent innumerable hours travelling within a two-to three-hour radius near my home in Winnipeg. It was terribly difficult to leave out some of my favourite images, like 'prairie abstract,' depicting a minimalist view of colour bands of wheat, grass, and sky, but we had earlier decided on a similar image for a double-page spread. Another favourite image that was left out illustrated a romantic, early-morning scene with lifting fog, but we already had a couple of images from that location. My criteria for selecting the images were based on quality, representation, variety, and season (to some extent), as well as how images worked together as a two-page spread and a section as a whole. Although the images were made over a period of thirty years, the vast majority of them were produced much more recently, within the last five to ten years. Both slide film and digital captures are included. Particular locations are featured more than once while others are not represented. Many images are now published for the first time in this book. Of paramount importance in selecting the images was capturing the spirit of the place rather than trying to represent every corner of the region.

In presenting such a body of work, I am always anxious to find the right person to write about the topic and, in so doing, complement my imagery in prose. Once again, I have found such a voice in Jan Volney. Jan introduces the various chapters by speaking to the landforms, the climate, the human culture, and the biology, including examples of the plants and animals found within the various habitats. He discusses issues such as climate change and nation building. Like the true ecologist he is, he understands profoundly how living organisms (including man) relate to their environment. His keen sense of observation enables him to offer great insight into the region.

As an artist, my focus in photography is to capture the beauty of this great country and to share it with others to remind us all of the importance that a healthy environment brings to the richness in our lives. The prairie has fascinated and inspired me for many years. I hope in turn to inspire you to get out and enjoy this most beautiful region of Canada.

—*Mike Grandmaison*

The Grasslands

The Prairies get their name from the vegetation of a triangular piece of geography ecologists call grasslands. In fact, 'prairie' is the French word used by early European settlers meaning grassland. One side of these grasslands is bounded by the 49th parallel. Ecologically this is an artificial boundary because these grassland ecosystems are part of a continental biome that stretches south to Texas. The western boundary runs north from the international border roughly parallel to the Rocky Mountain Foothills. Edmonton is at its apex, from which the irregular boundary runs almost southeast through Saskatchewan to a point just east of where the Red River flows into Manitoba. This grassland lies in the rain shadow of the Rocky Mountains wringing rains from weather systems travelling west from the Pacific Ocean before they reach the prairie.

As a result, the grasslands closest to the mountains are the driest in the region. The uplands are dominated by grasses such as rough fescue and forbs such as sticky geranium. To the east and stretching almost to the Saskatchewan/Manitoba border is the arid grassland most people think of as prairie. Needle-and-thread grass, blue grama grass, wheat grass, and june grass are the principal grasses here, while pasture sage and moss flox are common forbs. Cottonwoods and Manitoba maple (in Saskatchewan) occur on river terraces along with other trees and shrubs.

To the north and east of the more arid part of the grasslands lies a transitional area that merges into forest. A mosaic of trembling aspen groves and rough fescue grasslands characterizes plant communities in the western portion of this

1

transition zone. Toward the east, shrub communities join trembling aspen groves in moister sites, while bur oak appears in Manitoba.

The pronghorn, sage grouse, short-horned lizard, and western rattlesnake are characteristic wildlife of the true grassland, while in the transition zone there is a mixture of grassland and forest fauna including black bears.

The transitional grassland/forest that bounds the grassland region in the northeast lies roughly where there is barely enough precipitation to offset evaporation losses. However, the region still suffers from periodic droughts. Indeed, part of this grassland region is known as the Palliser Triangle. Droughts here are so frequent that the original surveys, by John Palliser, suggested that agriculture might not be feasible in this area. Irrigation was used to bring some of this land into agricultural production.

Grassland soils developed over bedrock as old mountain systems sent deposits into what used to be a shallow inland sea. The last Ice Age had a lasting impact on the landscapes we see today. As the ice sheet that covered the region 12,000 years ago moved under its own weight, it scoured the underlying land, sculpting it to a relatively level topography. Subsequent melting of the ice, the pooling of meltwaters

to create huge lakes at the ice margins, and the draining of these lakes left behind thick deposits of material that would evolve into the rich soils found over a large portion of the region today. These soils supported the grasses that eventually colonized the post-glacial landscapes, and they supported large populations of bison and other animals on which the original peoples would develop their culture. They would also attract settlers, however, who would eventually convert much of the land that was arable into highly productive farms. In the process, prairie landscapes would be completely transformed to become the breadbasket of the world, with the result that only a very small percentage of the original prairie remains undisturbed by the plough.

This transformation occurred over a spectacularly short time. Culturally the transformation would be equally spectacular. In the space of four decades, from about the 1880s, the settler population grew from a few tens of thousands to just over two million in 1921. The building of the transcontinental railway in Canada was seminal in more than one way. Many of the people it attracted remained as settlers. The railway was also the means of transportation of immigrants to the farms that were developing along its route and provided a means of transporting goods to the settlers and taking their produce to markets in eastern Canada and beyond and to western ports. It literally stitched the country together with that 'ribbon of steel.' But the railway system was more than a means of transport. It also imposed a pattern of settlement on the land. The villages, towns, and cities that were spurred to develop were sited so that farmers had roughly a half-day's cart ride to the nearest depot for shipping produce. That distance is about 13 km. Unlike in other areas of Canada, where water courses dictated settlement patterns, the railway really channelled the human influence on prairie landscapes. A special feature of several prairie settlements was the grain elevator built beside the tracks. It was natural for these locations to attract other businesses, such as restaurants and shops that would cater to farmers delivering their product to market. Today, several of these grain elevators remain and one can use them as beacons along the highway to indicate the approach of a village, long before the access road appears. Many wooden grain elevators have been abandoned, removed or destroyed. Those that remain are mainly museum pieces or put to different uses by some imaginative individual. Uniformly spaced along the tracks, they are being replaced with concrete structures at more infrequent junctures, since trucks can cover hundreds of kilometres in a few hours of driving.

One can expect that this region will see similar dramatic changes to the landscape in the near future. Three of the four fastest growing towns in Canada are found in the grassland region. Some of that growth is driven by the mining of potash deposits that were laid down by the ancient inland sea and are used in fertilizing agriculture in other countries. Additional growth is due to people coming from all over the world to work in the developing energy sector in nearby parts of the prairies. The population is also being transformed from its rural roots to one in which most people live in urban settings. These demographic changes will affect what happens in the near future, especially with the looming uncertainty as to what changes in climate will bring to this region. As the driest of regions in the Prairie provinces, this grassland system is probably where the effects of climate change will be felt most rapidly. One could expect that the grassland will expand north and agriculture will become increasingly difficult without irrigation in the southwest. Although the wooden grain elevator will disappear as a functioning part of the great agricultural system that developed in this grassland, some of its legacies are indelibly etched on the zone. For example, the grid road system and rectangular fields are a legacy of the township/range survey system used to allot land to settlers. And while the elevators may fade into time, the plaintive moan of the train's whistle can still be heard.

Overleaf: Wheat, canola, and sky
Notre Dame de Lourdes, MB

Above: The Qu'Appelle Valley
Near Grenfell, SK

The Qu'Appelle River
Buffalo Pound Provincial Park, SK

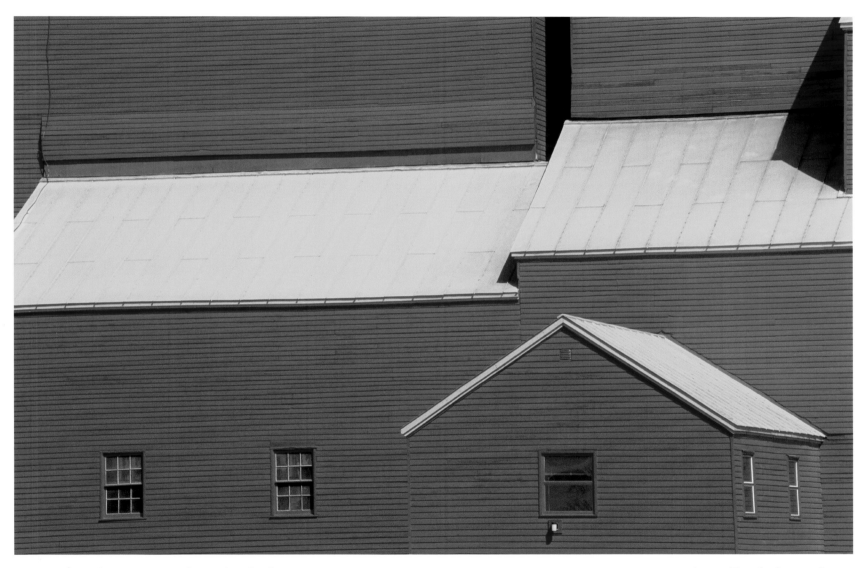

OPPOSITE: Wooden granaries and cumulus clouds
NEAR DELMAS, SK

ABOVE: Detail of grain elevator
LAJORD, SK

OPPOSITE: Swaths of canola
TROCHU, AB

ABOVE: Fields of blooming canola
NEAR HOLLAND, MB

Grain elevators and clouds
Mossleigh, AB

Abandoned Vauxhall car and church in ghost town
NEIDPATH, SK

Mature crop of wheat
Trochu, AB

Harvesting durum wheat
CARMICHAEL, SK

OPPOSITE: *Pattern of sunflowers*
TREHERNE, MB

ABOVE: *Undulating field of beans*
TREHERNE, MB

Flax, canola, and stormy sky
PORTAGE LA PRAIRIE, MB

TOP LEFT: *Swainson's hawk.* AVONLEA, SK
TOP RIGHT: *Snow geese.* BEECHY, SK
BOTTOM LEFT: *Canada geese.* OAK HAMMOCK MARSH, MB
BOTTOM RIGHT: *Western kingbird.* GRASSLANDS NATIONAL PARK (WEST BLOCK), SK

TOP LEFT: *American red squirrel.* WINNIPEG, MB
TOP RIGHT: *Richardson's ground squirrel.* OAK HAMMOCK MARSH, MB
BOTTOM LEFT: *Eastern cottontail rabbit.* WINNIPEG, MB
BOTTOM RIGHT: *Black-tailed prairie dog.* GRASSLANDS NATIONAL PARK (WEST BLOCK), SK

Red samphire at edge of slough
FOREMOST, AB

Field of three-flowered avens
Birds Hill Provincial Park, MB

Close-up of three-flowered avens
<small>BIRDS HILL PROVINCIAL PARK, MB</small>

Big bluestem in tall grass prairie
TOLSTOI TALL GRASS PRAIRIE PRESERVE, MB

Prairie crocus blossoms
Sandilands Provincial Forest, MB

25

ABOVE: *Asters*
GRASSLANDS NATIONAL PARK (WEST BLOCK), SK

OPPOSITE TOP: *Hereford cattle at sunset.* THREE HILLS, AB
OPPOSITE BOTTOM: *Pronghorns.* NEAR CYPRESS HILLS, AB

Bergamot flowers, sage, and flax field
PEMBINA VALLEY, MB

LEFT: Fringed gentian
MIDDLE: Western prairie fringed orchid
RIGHT: Meadow blazing star
TOLSTOI TALL GRASS PRAIRIE PRESERVE, MB

29

Sandstone outcrops
Roche Percee, SK

Autumn-coloured trembling aspen in a coulee
NEAR BENGOUGH, SK

Conglomerate Cliffs at sunrise
CYPRESS HILLS INTERPROVINCIAL PARK, SK

Sandstone concretion at sunrise
RED ROCK COULEE NATURAL AREA, AB

Hills of the grasslands
NEAR MAPLE CREEK, SK

Abandoned farmhouse at sunset
NEAR BRADDOCK, SK

Plains bison in last light
RIDING MOUNTAIN NATIONAL PARK, MB

Trees at sunrise
TOLSTOI TALL GRASS PRAIRIE PRESERVE, MB

OPPOSITE: *Stubble fields in winter*
MILO, AB

ABOVE: *Last light on cattails along the Seine River*
WINNIPEG, MB

OPPOSITE: Bales and Rocky Mountains in approaching storm. TWIN BUTTE, AB
ABOVE TOP: Horses in a snowstorm. NEAR MAPLE CREEK, SK
ABOVE BOTTOM: White-tailed deer in farmer's field. SOURIS, MB

43

Landscape covered in hoarfrost
BIRDS HILL PROVINCIAL PARK, MB

Red barn with hoarfrost
GRANDE POINTE, MB

OPPOSITE: *Qu'Appelle Valley at dawn*
NEAR CRAVEN, SK

ABOVE: *St. Nicholas Anglican Church*
NEAR CRAVEN, SK

General store at night
BENTS, SK

Full moon rising
STRATHMORE, AB

Valley of the Oldman River at sunset
NEAR PICTURE BUTTE, AB

Sun dogs
HEADINGLEY, MB

ABOVE: Willow tree in fog with hoarfrost
BIRDS HILL PROVINCIAL PARK, MB

OPPOSITE: A cold morning on the prairie
NEAR WILLOWS, SK

The Drylands

Characteristically, dryland areas of the Prairie provinces are dominated by their geology. They are often embedded in the more extensive grassland and occur in relatively small patches where moisture for plant growth is at a premium. Sandy areas and badlands are two dry landscape types found in the region. Ironically, badlands are formed by water from violent downpours penetrating and eroding hard surface rocks and eventually undermining lower, softer rock layers. This process produces steep-sided ravines and spurs. The vertical dimension of these landscapes prevents the accumulation and retention of what little water is available for runoff. On the other hand, moisture in sandy areas percolates through surface layers, bypassing the rooting zones of most plants.

One-fifth of land worldwide is desert and one-fifth of that is covered in sand. Sand, as opposed to dust and silt, is produced by erosion of sandstone and coarser rock fragments. The wind does a good job of sorting this material when it dries, leaving the heavier pebbles behind and blowing lighter dust and silt particles further along. The finer materials became the soils of much of the Prairie region. Where the wind blows over a sufficiently large accumulation of sand, dune systems often develop, probably seeded by an isolated pebble or other obstacle. It is not surprising, then, that the patterns we see in the shapes, orientation, and surfaces of dunes tell us something of the wind environments in which these land forms developed. Dunes in the Prairie provinces are the closest we will ever get to literally 'seeing the wind.'

In other regions of the world where the wind blows from the same direction all year long, crescent-shaped dunes form. However, dunes in the Prairie provinces do not take this shape since the wind blows from many different directions. The constant supply and movement of the sand particles, skipping up the shallow-sloped windward surface of dunes, builds the dune with a characteristically long windward tail. If the particle is blown over the crest, the lower wind speed on the leeward side deposits the grain, adding to the base for the next grain to build on. The leeward side of the dune is steeper than the windward side and is called the slip face. This is because when the dune reaches a certain height the face slumps onto the tail of the next dune. Movement of sand grains will propel dunes along the wind's direction. The progress of the dune is complex but limited by the source of the sand and the duration, direction, and speed of the wind. Its progress is one of growth, collapse, and renewal in response to the wind. With changeable winds, dunes appear to move around but remain largely confined to discrete pieces of land. Lighter winds produce ripples of sand that are essentially dunes in miniature. With sufficient rain, plants can get established on the dunes. They stabilize the sand and develop into plant communities, limiting the expansion of the system. If there is a return to drier condi-tions, the sand will start to move again. The Great Sand Hills in Saskatchewan, Spruce Woods Provincial Park, and the dunes on the northern shore of Lake Athabasca are all examples of these processes. Many of these dryland areas probably became established as sandy beaches at the margins of glacier lakes after the last Ice Age. Given the northern latitude and moisture regimes, most of them remain in limited areas where the advance of the vegetation is being held at bay by sand. Under present moist conditions, these dune systems cover relatively small areas, suggesting a shifting balance in favour of an advance of plant cover.

One of the most spectacular features of the badlands are the earth pillars known as hoodoos in the Prairie provinces. Typically, they have a hard rock cap that protects the 'body' from erosion by torrential downpours. Below this cap, the hoodoo body is made up of layers composed of softer materials such as clays and loose conglomerates incorporating rocks in the matrix. If the hoodoo loses its cap rock, for whatever reason, it is rapidly eroded by subsequent rains and disappears. The First Nations thought of them as petrified giants who came alive at night to hurl rocks at intruders. This is probably a reference to rocks falling off their bodies as hoodoos eroded. The French called them *demoiselles coiffées*, translated as 'ladies with hairdos,' because the cap rocks can be huge. These 'ladies' are found close to the valley wall where the surrounding land, unprotected from runoff, was eroded to leave the hoodoo isolated. The valley in which they form usually has a fast-moving river at its base to remove the products of erosion. The valley wall is fairly steep, sometimes almost vertical. Erosion is also evident on the wall with deep fissures running almost vertically from top to bottom. One can imagine new hoodoos emerging from the valley face.

Badlands are dynamic landscapes. They are a legacy of the sedimentary deposits formed in a shallow inland sea at the time of the dinosaurs. Wind, water, and the soft or unconsolidated nature of the sub-surface deposits with steep slopes now make for their rapid erosion. They are called 'badlands' because early peoples noted how difficult they were to travel through. If the area covered is large, one may even get lost in the intractable maze of gullies and spurs. Indeed, outlaws took advantage of this feature and used the Big Muddy Badlands as a hideout. Not all is bad about these landscapes, however. Fossils are frequently formed here and paleontologists have been richly rewarded in their exploration of these deposits. They are also a source of fossil fuel: coal. A visit to Drumheller, the badlands, and the Royal Tyrell Museum is well worth the effort to better appreciate the significance of these lands. While the deserts and badlands of the prairies might appear barren, plants, wildlife, and insect life have been able to survive in these dynamic environments. Many local animals are nocturnal and have special adaptations to conserve water in arid environments. Like most places castigated as 'bad,' they evoke a sense of mystery and reveal their secrets only to the daring.

It is remarkable that the diversity of ecological communities of the Prairie provinces should include dryland formations, given their abundant fresh-water reserves. It is not surprising, then, that the areas involved are small and occur in the dry parts of the west. But with a return to drier conditions we might expect these dryland formations to expand in area. These dry conditions have occurred before throughout the Prairie provinces. There are small pockets of grasslands and drylands located far to the north of the prairie zone. Cactus plants grow on the outskirts of Peace River, Alberta, some 500 km north of the prairie/forest boundary. This is a natural population growing in a relict grassland from an earlier dry period.

OVERLEAF: *Panorama of the grasslands with distant badlands*
GRASSLANDS NATIONAL PARK (EAST BLOCK), SK

ABOVE: *Castle Butte*
BIG MUDDY BADLANDS, SK

Milk River badlands at dusk
WRITING-ON-STONE PROVINCIAL PARK, AB

Sandstone formations in the Killdeer Badlands
GRASSLANDS NATIONAL PARK (EAST BLOCK), SK

Detail of badlands at sunset
LITTLE BOW PROVINCIAL PARK, AB

Milk River winding through the badlands
WRITING-ON-STONE PROVINCIAL PARK, AB

Twin hoodoos
WRITING-ON-STONE PROVINCIAL PARK, AB

Badlands
AVONLEA, SK

Badlands
WRITING-ON-STONE PROVINCIAL PARK, AB

Badlands
Dinosaur Provincial Park, AB

Intimate view of badlands
DINOSAUR PROVINCIAL PARK, AB

Badlands from the summit of Castle Butte
BIG MUDDY BADLANDS, SK

Valley along the Red Deer River
DRY ISLAND BUFFALO JUMP PROVINCIAL PARK, AB

ABOVE: *Killdeer Badlands*
GRASSLANDS NATIONAL PARK (EAST BLOCK), SK

OPPOSITE: *Detail of The Sandcastle*
NEAR BEECHY, SK

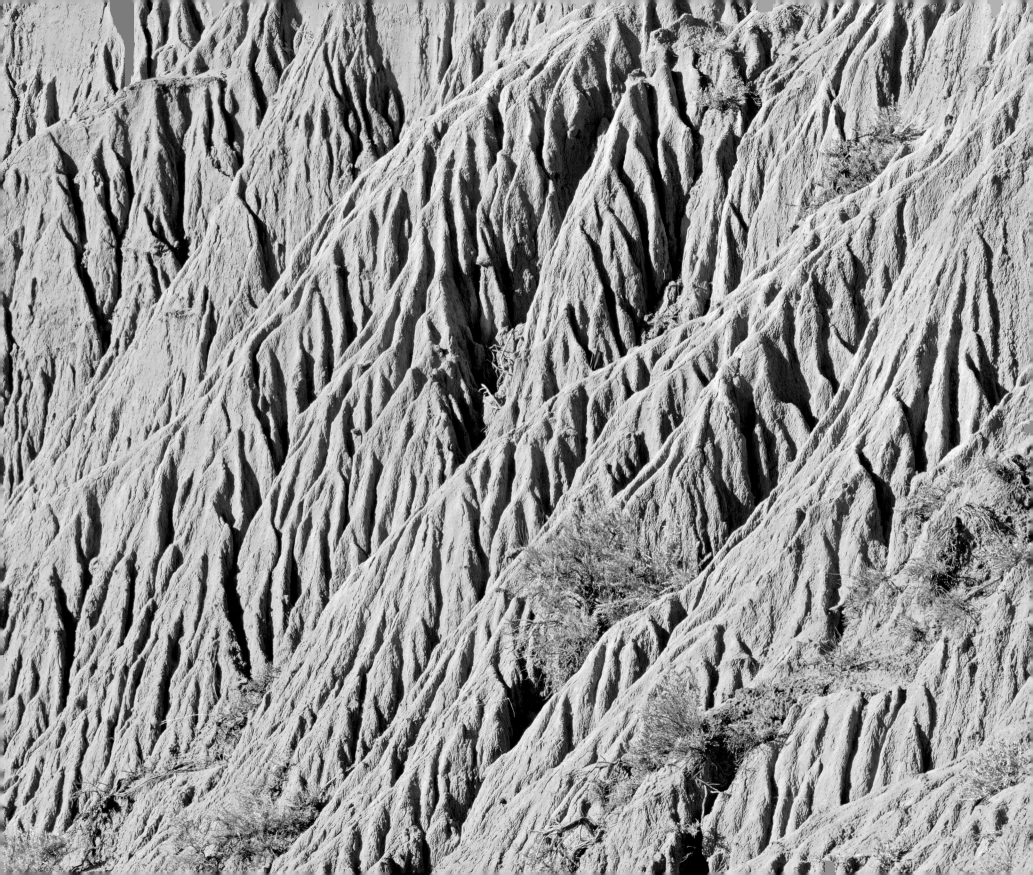

TOP LEFT: *Hoodoos. East Coulee, AB*
TOP RIGHT: *Hoodoo. Avonlea, SK*
BOTTOM LEFT: *Hoodoos. Writing-on-Stone Provincial Park, AB*
BOTTOM RIGHT: *Badlands. Dinosaur Provincial Park, AB*

Badlands in winter
EAST COULEE, AB

Badlands at sunset
DINOSAUR PROVINCIAL PARK, AB

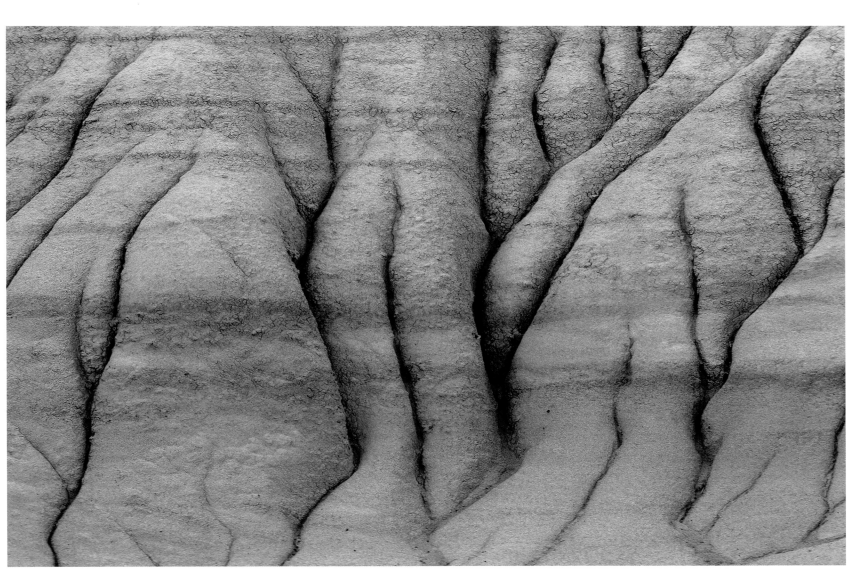

Detail of badlands in shade
DINOSAUR PROVINCIAL PARK, AB

Clouds at sunset
GREAT SAND HILLS, SK

Sand dunes at sunset
GREAT SAND HILLS, SK

Ripples in sand
GREAT SAND HILLS, SK

Ripples on dune face
GREAT SAND HILLS, SK

Prairie sunflowers in the Carberry Desert at sunrise
SPRUCE WOODS PROVINCIAL PARK, MB

Prairie sunflowers in the Carberry Desert
SPRUCE WOODS PROVINCIAL PARK, MB

Sand pattern on dune #1
GREAT SAND HILLS, SK

Sand pattern on dune #2
GREAT SAND HILLS, SK

Sand dune face and cloud
GREAT SAND HILLS, SK

OPPOSITE TOP LEFT: Sand hoodoos. GREAT SAND HILLS, SK
OPPOSITE TOP RIGHT: Sand hoodoos. GREAT SAND HILLS, SK
OPPOSITE MIDDLE LEFT: Dried plant remains in sand. JASPER NATIONAL PARK, AB
OPPOSITE MIDDLE RIGHT: Horsetails in sand. JASPER NATIONAL PARK, AB
OPPOSITE BOTTOM LEFT: Pattern on sandy beach. LESSER SLAVE LAKE PROVINCIAL PARK, AB
OPPOSITE BOTTOM RIGHT: Plants and animal tracks in sand. GREAT SAND HILLS, SK

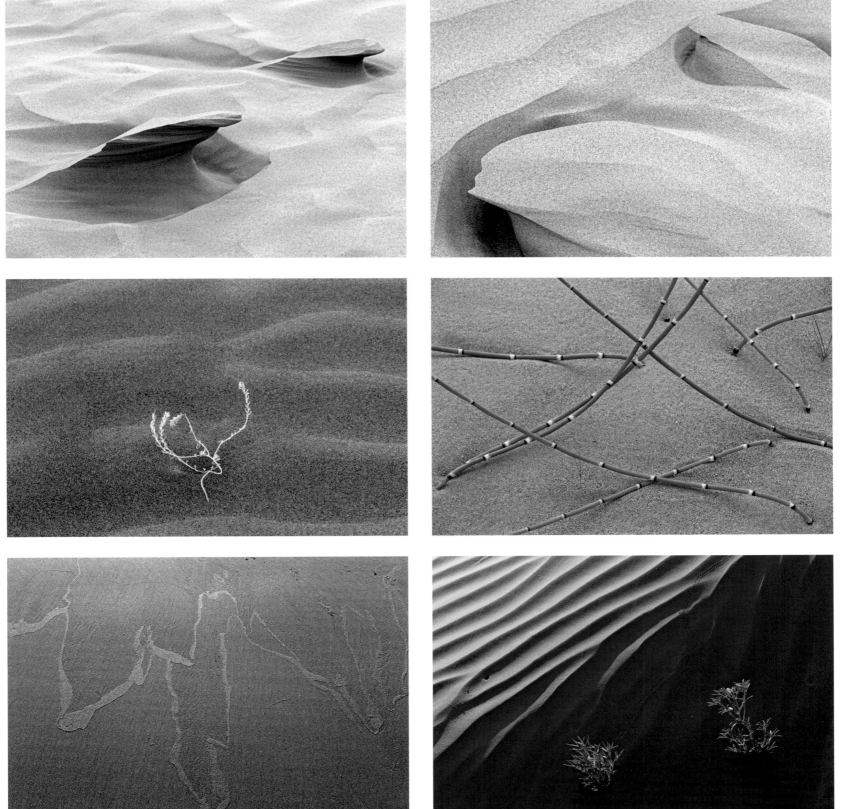

The Forests

The Boreal Forest Region is a transcontinental vegetation belt stretching from Newfoundland to Alaska. Across the Prairie provinces, the boreal forest is characterized by white and black spruces with admixtures of tamarack. Balsam fir and jack pine may be found from central Alberta east into Manitoba. In the foothills forests of Alberta, these two species are replaced by lodgepole pine and subalpine fir. In extreme southwestern Alberta, montane and subalpine forests border the prairie. Although primarily a coniferous forest, trembling aspen and balsam poplar, which are broad-leaved, are important elements of the boreal forest, especially in the transition area north of the prairie. Towards the north, as soil and climate conditions become harsher, black spruce and tamarack become more dominant as the closed-canopied forest gives way to open woodlands of the Subarctic. In southeastern Manitoba, the boreal transitions to the Great Lakes–St. Lawrence Forest Region. The area east of the Sandilands Provincial Forest includes species common in the latter, such as elm, basswood, Manitoba maple, and bur oak. To the south the boreal forest gives way to the grasslands.

The boreal forest of the Prairie provinces provides important winter range for caribou. It is also home to many fur-bearing animals, including black bear, lynx, moose, wolf, snowshoe hare, and spruce grouse. Ruffed grouse and Canada goose, together with other waterfowl, are often hunted in the region. Sadly, local populations of bison, sandhill, and whooping cranes are significant species of concern.

Opposite: Autumn in the aspen parkland
Riding Mountain National Park, MB

The most spectacular characteristic of the boreal forests of the Prairie provinces is that they are adapted to natural disturbances. Only a few tree generations ago the area now occupied by the boreal forest was laid waste by one such disturbance, the glacier of the last Ice Age. The plants and animals that colonized post-glacial environments had adaptations that allowed them to become established and thrive in essentially barren lands. These would include reproductive (wind dispersal of seed), survival (rapid growth to occupy sites), and coping strategies (partitioning of resources to compete with other species) that permitted them to dominate new environments following the retreat of the glaciers. In the process of colonizing these new lands they also ameliorated the local environment for the species that would follow and further enrich the communities. Along with fluctuations in climate, the species that have survived in this area are thus adapted to catastrophic change.

Climatic conditions in the region now occupied by the boreal forest have put a premium on species that can survive in fire-prone environments. Stand-replacing fires recreate some features of this early environment. Aspen is able to rapidly recolonize burned areas, either through seeding or sprouting from the pre-existing stand. Once established, aspens become deep rooted and grow rapidly to occupy an area. The trees now produce an annual crop of leaf litter, twigs, and other woody material that is acted on by a variety of insects and their ilk, together with fungi and other micro-organisms, to move the organic material into the forest floor and improve soil conditions. Winged seeds blown in from nearby mature white spruce trees eventually become established and form a mixed-wood stand. But the trees are adapted to avoid competition early in stand development: spruce is shallow rooted, whereas aspen is deeper rooted. Spruce trees are evergreen, so their development as an understory tree in aspen stands permits them to take advantage of light penetrating the lower canopy for rapid growth on warm spring and fall days when leaves are off the aspens. Shade provided by the canopy keeps the tops of spruce trees cool, largely protecting them from damage by a terminal weevil, active in summers, which would otherwise interfere with normal height growth. Spruce trees ultimately penetrate the canopy, the shorter-lived aspen stems start to die, and spruce trees come to dominate the stand. However, there are almost always a few long-lived aspen stems that maintain a presence in these stands to maintain and nurture their vast root system. Should an intense fire occur, this deep network of roots now yields its payoff for aspen. Spruce, being less tolerant of fire, now yields the field to aspen. In the spring, heat from the sun on the blackened soil surface initiates sprouting by aspen roots to regenerate an aspen stand. This process can be repeated on a site indefinitely. The time from regenerating an aspen stand to domination of the site by white spruce may take one or two centuries. At any point fire may intervene to reset the succession of stands at a particular site to initiate a wave of aspen regeneration from sprouts. The phrase 'phoenix forest' is justly applied to this type of regenerated forest.

Insects also cause disturbance in these forests. The forest tent caterpillar feeds on aspen in the boreal forest. White spruce and balsam fir trees are often damaged by outbreaks of spruce budworm populations. The insect damages and kills balsam fir preferentially, giving white spruce an advantage over its competitor in this region. Occasionally tree mortality in mixed balsam fir/white spruce stands is such that the elevated fuel load within stands increases the risk of stand-replacing fires. It would appear that exclusion of balsam fir by white spruce mediated by the insect is to the latter's advantage in sustaining its dominance of a site. The insect thus serves to render white spruce a competitive advantage. The mountain pine beetle poses a new threat to forests in the boreal region. The insect is capable of surviving in jack pine, whose range extends across the continent. However, whether the mountain pine beetle can thrive in climates where jack pine grows remains unknown.

Much of the transition between the grassland and forest in the boreal region has been cleared for agriculture and settlement, leaving isolated remnants of stands and some riparian forests intact. The boreal forest itself is indirectly vulnerable to human activities, affecting changes in climate and global geochemical cycles such as water, carbon, and nitrogen cycles. The direct effects on the forest are caused by local unsustainable forestry practices. Fortunately, there is hope. Many forest companies have abandoned clear-cutting in favour of 'variable retention forestry.' In contrast to clear-cutting, stands that are harvested retain green trees distributed in patterns that conserve all, if not most, species on the landscape. Un-harvested patches serve to 'life-boat' animal, plant, and micro-organism populations so that they can disperse and colonize into the disturbed areas. This should allow all populations to regenerate more rapidly than they would have in large clear-cut areas. Although the jury is still out on the efficacy of this harvest system, arguably the world's largest fully replicated forest science experiment to test just this hypothesis is located in the Boreal Forest Region in Alberta. This experiment has started to yield encouraging results on the sustainability of stands harvested in this fashion.

OVERLEAF: Mixedwood forest in autumn colours
NEAR DUNVEGAN, AB

ABOVE: Aspen trees in early autumn
PRINCE ALBERT NATIONAL PARK, SK

*Worm's eye view of aspen
trees in autumn splendour*
PRINCE ALBERT NATIONAL PARK, SK

95

Eastern larches (tamarack) reflected in the Lily Pond
WHITESHELL PROVINCIAL PARK, MB

TOP LEFT: *White-tailed deer.* PRINCE ALBERT NATIONAL PARK, SK
TOP RIGHT: *American black bear sow and cub.* PRINCE ALBERT NATIONAL PARK, SK
BOTTOM LEFT: *Coyote.* ELK ISLAND NATIONAL PARK, AB
BOTTOM RIGHT: *American porcupine.* ELK ISLAND NATIONAL PARK, AB

Aspen trees in Bois-des-Esprits in the Seine River forest
WINNIPEG, MB

TOP LEFT: *Large yellow lady's-slipper.* WHITESHELL PROVINCIAL PARK, MB
TOP RIGHT: *Aspen leaves in autumn colour.* WHITESHELL PROVINCIAL PARK, MB
BOTTOM LEFT: *Mushrooms (Order Agaricales).* WHITESHELL PROVINCIAL PARK, MB
BOTTOM RIGHT: *Club moss after a fire.* COWAN, MB

Fogbow over mixedwood forest
WHITESHELL PROVINCIAL PARK, MB

Double rainbow over forest
YORKTON, SK

Last light on boreal forest
CLEARWATER LAKE PROVINCIAL PARK, MB

102

Trees in fog at Lyons Lake
WHITESHELL PROVINCIAL PARK, MB

Aspen trees reflected in creek at sunset
WHITESHELL PROVINCIAL PARK, MB

104

Last light on aspen trees
DUCK MOUNTAIN PROVINCIAL PARK, MB

Great grey owl in spruce tree
NEAR THE PAS, MB

Forest floor covered in lichens
LEAF RAPIDS, MB

Aspen trees in rain
RIDING MOUNTAIN NATIONAL PARK, MB

Backlit coniferous trees
NOPIMING PROVINCIAL PARK, MB

Charred trees in recent burn
NEAR ASHERN, MB

Frost-covered forest floor
WHITESHELL PROVINCIAL PARK, MB

LEFT: *Ram's-head lady's-slipper.* GYPSUMVILLE, MB
MIDDLE: *Small round-leaved orchid.* NEAR ZHODA, MB
RIGHT: *Small purple fringed orchid.* NEAR BUFFALO POINT, MB

Spruce tree trunks at sunset
DUCK MOUNTAIN PROVINCIAL PARK, MB

Dogwood twigs and lichen-covered rock
WHITESHELL PROVINCIAL PARK, MB

Dogwood leaves and berries in autumn
BISSETT, MB

Rainbow over road
PRINCE ALBERT NATIONAL PARK, SK

Late afternoon light streaking through coniferous forest
PISEW FALLS PROVINCIAL PARK, MB

Hoarfrost and new snow on a cold morning
PISEW FALLS PROVINCIAL PARK, MB

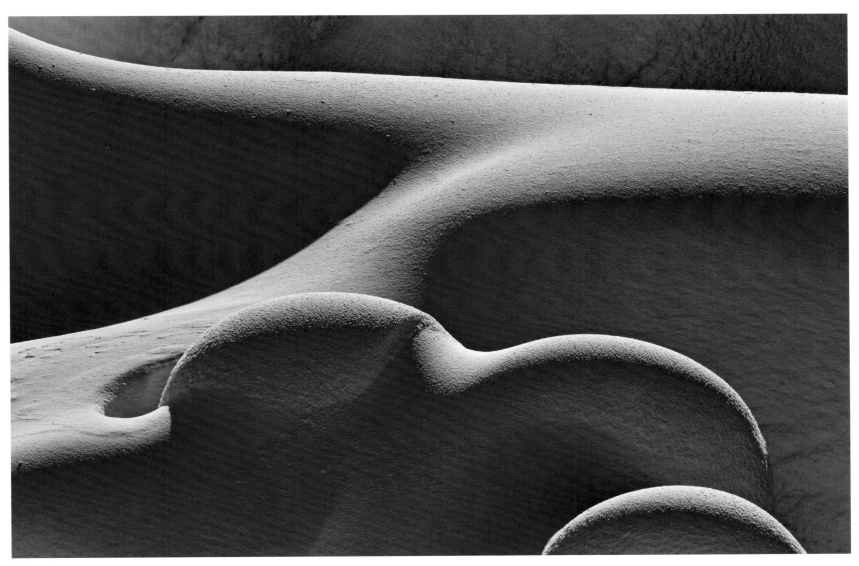

Mounds of snow near Pisew Falls
PISEW FALLS PROVINCIAL PARK, MB

119

Hoarfrost-covered trees
BIRDS HILL PROVINCIAL PARK, MB

White spruce trees covered in hoarfrost
BIRDS HILL PROVINCIAL PARK, MB

Sunset in St. Vital Park after a snowfall
WINNIPEG, MB

122

Last light on snowy trees in St. Vital Park
Winnipeg, MB

Star trails and jack pine forest
SANDILANDS PROVINCIAL FOREST, MB

Northern lights display above white spruce trees
BIRDS HILL PROVINCIAL PARK, MB

The Wetlands

The rivers that water the Prairie provinces originate from two general sources. Two of the major river systems begin as glacier-fed streams high in the Rocky Mountains on the continental divide that marks the western border of the region. These are the Saskatchewan River and Athabasca — Peace River systems. The former ends its journey in Lake Winnipeg, where its water in turn crosses the Canadian Shield to drain into Hudson Bay. The Athabasca and Peace Rivers lose their identities as they enter the Peace-Athabasca delta and feed Lake Athabasca. These waters flow into the Northwest Territories and eventually meet the Arctic Ocean. Except for their flow out of the mountains, both river systems travel across a great sedimentary basin, a remnant of an ancient inland sea dating back to the time of the dinosaurs. These rivers make their way toward the oceans, picking up silt from the variety of glacial deposits and soft sedimentary rocks of their basins. Before they reach the Shield their water is seldom clear. Water from annual precipitation to river basins complements these flows.

The other general source for the remaining river systems comes from annual precipitation inputs. The Red River that flows north to Lake Winnipeg from the United States relies exclusively on these inputs. It too, along with its tributaries, carries heavy sediment loads throughout its course. The Churchill River system also depends on annual precipitation inputs, but it flows mainly across the hard rocks of the Canadian Shield, picking up little sediment in the process, before draining into Hudson Bay. The rivers that cross the Shield might be best described as consisting of a string of lakes. As a result, sediments transported by the flow would be deposited in what amounts to settling basins, and these waters appear clear. The colour may be altered by the soluble organic matter picked up by flowing through peat wetlands to that of tea. In general, the big lakes of the region (Lakes Athabasca, Winnipeg, Manitoba), like the Great Lakes of central Canada and Great Slave and Great Bear Lakes of the Northwest Territories, lie at the boundary between the Canadian Shield and the inland sedimentary basin. Deltas often form where the silt-bearing rivers lose their momentum as they enter the lakes. These deltas are some of the most productive areas in the world for waterfowl and other wildlife species. Except for the headwaters of the mountain streams, the major rivers flow over a shallow gradient with few major waterfalls, minimizing the number of portages required during river travel. The Shield acts as a barrier to water flow over a considerable area of land at its entire margin in the Prairie provinces.

Significantly, about one-quarter of the land area in the Prairie provinces is covered by natural wetlands. These are places where the land remains waterlogged most of the time. The extent of wetlands in the region results from the gentle slope of the terrain, permitting pooling and slow water movement, especially at the areas immediately adjacent to the Canadian Shield. Wetlands go by various names such as bogs, moors, mires, muskeg, and sloughs, and ecologists recognize no fewer than 70 different wetland forms in Canada. Each form may harbour a distinctly different vegetation community and associated wildlife. Some have accumulated large deposits of carbon in the form of peat, all deposited since the melting of glaciers less than 10,000 years ago. Ominously, they are prevented from releasing this carbon in the form of greenhouse gases as long as they remain waterlogged in their cold northern environments. Some of the strangest plants may be found in bogs. For example, pitcher plants that grow in nutrient-poor waters of peat bogs must rely on decaying insects trapped in their 'pitchers' to obtain nitrogen and other nutrients for growth.

The story of this continental water system would not be complete, however, without mention of a significant biological element with profound impacts on the history of the area.

I doubt that any other animal has had the geopolitical impact that the beaver has had in shaping the modern world. This all stemmed from the value Europeans placed on its fur in the 18th and 19th centuries. The inland network of water bodies proved providential for the fur-trading companies in pursuit of their quarry: the beaver and other fur-bearers. In a very real sense the wealth that was extracted from what Europeans originally called Rupert's Land was largely dependent on the lakes, rivers, and wetlands of this part of the continent.

The beaver is legitimately the star of this story. It builds dams of mud, cementing together logs from trees it fells using its incisors. These dams are built across creeks impounding water that floods adjacent lands. The beavers then have access to more trees for dam construction which further expands their wetland habitat. The animals live in lodges, also constructed from mud and wood, surrounded by water and located well behind the dams. Presumably this provides insurance against destruction of the lodges in case their dams are breached by high water levels, and to avoid raids by terrestrial predators. These dams are marvels of engineering; they are almost always curved, not unlike the large dams built at hydroelectricity-generating facilities, and can be quite large. One beaver dam in northeastern Alberta is more than a kilometre long. There are several similar large dams in the area where a sequence of their impoundments have visibly altered the flow of water. Unfortunately for the beaver, the fur trade also exploited these water courses in trapping the animals. The larger water bodies provided the means of transportation of the pelts for exchange at the fur-trading company forts in return for manufactured European goods. The canoe was the vessel of choice for the short-haul journeys to the various fur-trading forts. From the fort, specially designed York boats would take the pelts to Hudson Bay for trans-shipment in Europe-bound ocean-going ships. Today, few beavers are trapped because demand for pelts has collapsed. Populations have recovered to such an extent that they have become a nuisance to engineers by their interference with culverts designed to keep water away from roads at creek crossings. Nevertheless, they continue to have impacts on the wetland landscape.

The extent and diversity of the wetlands throughout the Prairie provinces, particularly in the boreal region, have restricted all-weather road construction in this area. Ice roads have been developed to permit winter travel so as to overcome the isolation of northern communities. More recently, industrial forestry uses ice roads to extract timber that would otherwise be inaccessible in northern areas. Climate change will bring new challenges to the region. As the ice-free season grows ever longer, ice roads will become increasingly difficult to construct and maintain. Precipitation patterns will change and alter the supply of water to create demands for an increasingly growing human population. Attempts at managing this water supply, such as inter-basin transfers of water, will bring significant changes to wildlife populations (including fisheries) dependent on the various wetlands and water bodies of the region. Most significantly, the drying and warming of wetlands could expel untold volumes of greenhouse gases, leading to further drying and warming.

OVERLEAF: *Sunrise on Astotin Lake* | ABOVE: *Morning fog on the Winnipeg River*
ELK ISLAND NATIONAL PARK, AB | LAC DU BONNET, MB

Reeds at sunrise
DUCK MOUNTAIN PROVINCIAL PARK, MB

Storm brewing over Lesser Slave Lake
LESSER SLAVE LAKE PROVINCIAL PARK, AB

Common mergansers on shore of Rainbow Falls
WHITESHELL PROVINCIAL PARK, MB

Dawn on oxbow of the Spruce River
PRINCE ALBERT NATIONAL PARK, SK

136

Grasses reflected in waters of the Spruce River
PRINCE ALBERT NATIONAL PARK, SK

OPPOSITE: Morning frost on the shore of the La Salle River
LA BARRIÈRE PROVINCIAL PARK, MB

ABOVE: Trees reflected in pond
ELK ISLAND NATIONAL PARK, AB

Dawn on Clear Lake
RIDING MOUNTAIN NATIONAL PARK, MB

TOP LEFT: *Franklin's gull.* BUFFALO POUND PROVINCIAL PARK, SK
TOP RIGHT: *American white pelican.* FAIRFORD, MB
BOTTOM LEFT: *Eared grebes.* SOMERSET, MB
BOTTOM RIGHT: *Ring-billed gulls.* WHITESHELL PROVINCIAL PARK, MB

OPPOSITE: *Leopard frog on water lily in Assiniboine Park*
WINNIPEG, MB

ABOVE: *Water smartweed*
ORKNEY, SK

143

Northern lights over pier of Lake Winnipeg
MATLOCK, MB

Yellow water lilies on Lily Pond
WHITESHELL PROVINCIAL PARK, MB

146

Blue flag iris
WHITESHELL PROVINCIAL PARK, MB

Pattern of reeds on Athapapuskow Lake
BAKERS NARROWS, MB

White Lake reflection
NEAR FLIN FLON, MB

McGillivray Falls
WHITESHELL PROVINCIAL PARK, MB

149

Bird River at Tulabi Falls
NOPIMING PROVINCIAL PARK, MB

Detail of Bird River at Tulabi Falls
NOPIMING PROVINCIAL PARK, MB

Detail of Rainbow Falls
WHITESHELL PROVINCIAL PARK, MB

Rainbow Falls empties into White Lake
WHITESHELL PROVINCIAL PARK, MB

Partial rainbow over Waskesiu Lake
PRINCE ALBERT NATIONAL PARK, SK

Evening light on shore of Little Limestone Lake
Near Grand Rapids, MB

OPPOSITE: *Pier on Lake Winnipeg at dawn*
MATLOCK, MB

ABOVE: *Morning reflection of clouds on Namekus Lake*
PRINCE ALBERT NATIONAL PARK, SK

Clouds reflected in prairie slough at sunrise
GRANDE PRAIRIE, AB

Limestone cliffs along the shore of Lake Manitoba
STEEP ROCK, MB

Dusk on Lesser Slave Lake
LESSER SLAVE LAKE PROVINCIAL PARK, AB

Evening light over Sasagiu Rapids
SASAGIU RAPIDS, MB

Spring ice along Lake Winnipeg
WINNIPEG BEACH, MB

Detail of ice on Clear Lake
RIDING MOUNTAIN NATIONAL PARK, MB

The Mountains

Some of the most beautiful landscapes in the world are to be found in the Rocky Mountain National Parks of Canada. With many peaks over 3000 metres high, the continental divide along the crest of the Rocky Mountains forms the southwestern boundary of the Prairie provinces. At these latitudes, these peaks are flanked by glaciers and may be covered by snow year round. This western mountain spine has had a significant influence on many aspects of the physical geography of the Prairie provinces.

A trip through Banff and Jasper National Parks along the Icefields Parkway furnishes the best lesson on glacial geology anywhere. The valleys west of the divide have been sculpted more by water than by ice and have developed a V-shaped cross section. In contrast, valleys on the east side, lying on the colder side in the rain shadow of winds from the west, have been worked to a greater extent by glaciers than have their western counterparts. These valleys develop the classic U-shaped cross section, with almost vertical sides and wide valley bottoms, affording a larger view of the sky. The peaks are also shaped by glaciers. On their shoulders might be cirques: the punchbowl-shaped depressions that seem to retain remnants of a glacier or its meltwater. If these cirques develop on several sides of a peak and their margins meet, a 'horn' or sharp peak is formed. A 'perched valley,' usually ending in a waterfall, develops where a tributary glacier intersects a U-shaped valley high on its wall and seems to hang way above the valley floor. The Angel Glacier in Jasper National Park is a spectacular example where, instead of a waterfall, the body and wings of the 'angel' are glaciers. Truncated spurs punctuate the spaces between these tributary valleys. The Athabasca Glacier, part of the huge Columbia Icefield, is now accessible by the Parkway. To walk from the parking area to its toe is to witness the impacts of a glacier on the terrain, the meltwater, and, now, the effects of climate change on the recession of the ice sheet. First there is the rubble that resulted from the glacier's advance scouring its bed and depositing this material in the form of moraines. The terminal moraine, marking the furthest advance of the ice sheet, forms a dam of rubble across the valley. This dam is breached by meltwater to form a braided stream. If not breached, these moraines will impound a meltwater lake. One such 'moraine lake' used to be featured on Canadian 20-dollar bills. The meltwater is often laden with silt, but when the larger particles settle in lakes or slower-moving water bodies, the finer particles are left suspended in the water. This is known as rock flour, and its suspension in water gives a characteristic greenish colour to the lakes and rivers associated with these glaciers.

From a distance, the vegetation appears to be stratified into zones. On the highest peaks and ridges of the mountains few plants can grow where the environment is the harshest.

Below the high alpine zone, isolated shrubs and stunted trees together with some herbaceous plant species cling to a precarious existence on the margins of life's tolerance to extremes. Lower still, one sees an accumulation of larger shrubs and trees where the environment is more benign and plants have established a genuine foothold on the land. Eventually, fully developed forests that look and feel like the boreal forest dominate the landscape. Grasslands may also occur in locations where moisture is at a premium. Each plant species has a niche in which it will thrive best. This is often related to its tolerance of the local climate. As a consequence, communities develop as belts on these mountain slopes in response to elevational changes in temperature regimes. But the pattern is never that simple. The mosaic of communities, best witnessed in the fall when plants are modifying their leaf colours, tells a story of disturbance, successful regeneration, development, and survival of communities. Larches, trembling aspen, willows, and a host of shrubs go through a predictable seasonal pattern of kaleidoscopic colour changes. By contrast the evergreens, lodgepole pine, Engelmann spruce, and subalpine fir are more subtle in their seasonal colour change. Rock falls, avalanches, fires, and insect outbreaks all play a role in configuring the patterns we see on these mountain slopes. In a sense, the vegetation zones we see as we ascend in altitude mimic the zones as we ascend in latitude. The advantage we find in the mountains is that the change occurs over relatively short horizontal distances.

Often hidden from view but important to the ecosystem is the myriad of wildlife species that inhabit mountain regions. The mountain parks serve a valuable conservation role because several rare species find refuge and protection there. Grizzly bear, bighorn sheep, mountain goat, wolverine, cougar, and pika are characteristic wildlife in the parks. To this we may add elk, many of which have been herded into the townsites to avoid predation. The harlequin duck in Jasper National Park is one of the more colourful bird species that can be seen in western Canada. Steller's jay, a species commonly found west of the continental divide, adds diversity to the visual feast that is these parks.

The near pristine environments in most areas have become an attraction to those seeking spiritual solace from the day-to-day concerns of an increasingly urban population. There is now increasing concern that some of the impacts on threatened and endangered species in this region might extirpate them from this part of their range. Principal among these is the woodland caribou, which is sensitive to habitat loss and predation as a consequence of land use changes in lands adjacent to the parks. Although there is some watershed management in the foothills, the most serious regional demand from a human perspective has to do with water. In a real sense, these mountains and the glacier-fed rivers provide vital succor to the lands that now support some of the fastest growing cities in Canada. The major cities in the Prairie provinces are in the rain shadow of these mountains. Precipitation in the region alone cannot sustain the increasing water needs of the human population. The accelerated melting of glaciers in the icefields indicates a new challenge. That is: how do we manage sustainably all aspects of the resources flowing from these mountains?

Last light on the peaks of the Colin Range at Medicine Lake
JASPER NATIONAL PARK, AB

Dawn on Waterton Lake
WATERTON LAKES NATIONAL PARK, AB

Icebergs at Mt. Edith Cavell at sunrise
JASPER NATIONAL PARK, AB

Early morning clouds reflected in Herbert Lake
BANFF NATIONAL PARK, AB

Mountain peak shining through fog at first light
JASPER NATIONAL PARK, AB

Mt. Rundle and clouds reflected in Vermilion Lakes at dawn
BANFF NATIONAL PARK, AB

Pyramid Mountain reflected in Patricia Lake at sunrise
Jasper National Park, AB

Canadian Rocky Mountains reflected in wetland along the Icefields Parkway near Bow Summit
BANFF NATIONAL PARK, AB

Whirlpool Peak, Mt. Fryatt, and Leech Lake
JASPER NATIONAL PARK, AB

Classic view of Peyto Lake
BANFF NATIONAL PARK, AB

Moraine Lake and the Valley of the Ten Peaks
Banff National Park, AB

Lake Louise reflection
BANFF NATIONAL PARK, AB

Crowfoot Mountain reflected in Bow Lake
BANFF NATIONAL PARK, AB

Rock face reflected in Horseshoe Lake
JASPER NATIONAL PARK, AB

181

182

*Bow River with Castle Mountain
in the background*
BANFF NATIONAL PARK, AB

Bull elk bugling
JASPER NATIONAL PARK, AB

Waterfall in Maligne Canyon
JASPER NATIONAL PARK, AB

Cameron Falls
WATERTON LAKES NATIONAL PARK, AB

185

The Canadian Rocky Mountains in autumn
ALONG THE DAVID THOMPSON HIGHWAY, AB

Aspen turning colour in early autumn
ALONG THE DAVID THOMPSON HIGHWAY, AB

Spillway Lake in autumn
Kananaskis Country, AB

Alpine meadows in early autumn near Highwood Pass
KANANASKIS COUNTRY, AB

Mountain peak and western larches (tamarack) in autumn colour
KANANASKIS COUNTRY, AB

Top left: *Bighorn sheep.* Jasper National Park, AB
Top right: *Grizzly bear.* Banff National Park, AB
Bottom left: *Mountain goat.* Jasper National Park, AB
Bottom right: *American black bear sow and cubs.* Banff National Park, AB

Bow River and fog
BANFF NATIONAL PARK, AB

192

Low-level clouds and mountain peak
Jasper National Park, AB

Sun gently lighting up the alpine zone
KANANASKIS COUNTRY, AB

ABOVE: *Detail of the peak at Pyramid Mountain*
JASPER NATIONAL PARK, AB

OVERLEAF: *Cow moose and calf sauntering along Medicine Lake*
JASPER NATIONAL PARK, AB

The Subarctic

Environments in the Subarctic mirror several features of the Rocky Mountains which lie 1600 km southwest of Manitoba's northern border on the Hudson Bay coast. Lands adjacent to this most northerly coast are classified as part of the Low Arctic. Although this is the largest eco-climatic region in Canada, the area in Manitoba is limited to about 3200 sq km. Short, cool summers with the risk of frost ever present mean that the frozen soils can do little better than support true tundra. This is a vegetation type in which plants are dwarfed or stunted. Dwarf birch may reach a height of only 2 m. An area of continuous permafrost extends beyond the Low Arctic south along the entire length of bay-shore in Manitoba. Inland from this is a belt where open-grown black spruce with an understory of dwarf birch,

Labrador tea, and lichens can develop on upland sites. On poorly drained areas, a sequence of bogs and fens often develop. In bogs, black spruce, Labrador tea, bog rosemary, and cloudberry grow on the wet carpet of sphagnum moss. On fens, where plant nutrient concentrations in the water are higher than that in bogs, sedges, and reeds can also be found. Trees growing in these environments are often also stunted and sparsely distributed. They may, however, develop as closed canopied stands in more southerly areas protected from the worst effects of the northern environment. This area is part of the Subarctic Ecoclimatic Region that stretches northwesterly from the Ontario/Manitoba border to the Saskatchewan/Northwest Territories boundary north of Lake Athabasca. A place of discontinuous permafrost, it

OPPOSITE: *Last light on treeline*
CHURCHILL, *MB*

is common to find what can be best described as 'drunken forests.' Trees that grow on permafrost eventually reach a height where they become top-heavy. When the permafrost melts the trees start to lean at the least disturbance because their shallow root systems are unable to support the above-ground structures. Not all trees lean in the same direction so that the impression is one of trees that have lost their 'sense of balance' to 'stagger.' Much of the area west of the Hudson Bay lowlands is on the Canadian Shield. The vegetation is described as 'forest and barren.' These barrens occur where there is virtually no soil because the landscape was scoured bare by the last advance of an ancient ice sheet.

We can still see the effects of the several-kilometres-thick ice sheet on the land. Ice at the base of the sheet would flow under its own weight, carrying rocks and finer debris to rake any soil off the land. Not being confined to valleys over this flat terrain as the mountain glaciers were, they spread out as a vast apron of ice across Canada east of the Rocky Mountains to latitudes of melt south of the 49th parallel. The weight of this ice on the landscape was sufficient to depress the Canadian Shield into the earth's mantle, well below its pre-glacial elevation. As the ice melted this pressure was reduced and the Shield started to rise. Geologists call this process isostatic rebound. Today the bedrock is rising at the rate of about 1 cm per year. If this is correct, the base of stone structures, such as Prince of Wales Fort on Hudson Bay, built in the 18th century, would be about 2.5 m higher above sea level now than when they were built. The melting and hydraulic action of the rushing glacial meltwater completed the process of rendering patches of the landscape barren, denuded of any soil, and vegetation that occupied the area prior to glaciation. The Canadian Shield in this part of the Subarctic was liberated from this prison of ice only about 9,000 years ago, essentially resetting the ecosystem development back to zero. Since then, a maximum of 30 to 60 generations of trees could have occupied these sites if they were growing at rates we observe today. In terms of ecosystem evolution, this is a comparatively young community, developing novel ecological relationships while adapting to the new assortment of species that have managed to colonize the area.

The human population in this region has always been sparse and mainly transient. The first permanent European settlement on what we now know as the Prairie provinces of Canada began on the Hudson Bay coast. On May 2, 1670, The Governor and Company of Adventurers of England trading into Hudson's Bay (known today as the Hudson's Bay Company) was granted a charter to exclusive fur-trading rights to all lands drained by rivers flowing into Hudson

Bay. One of the surviving relicts of this era is Prince of Wales Fort near Churchill, Manitoba. Geopolitically, locating a fort at the mouth of the Churchill River was strategic: it initially avoided competition with the French trading out of New France; it established a short shipping route from Europe to the centre of the North American continent as well as access to an abundant resource that ultimately broke the Russian fur trade monopoly; it secured access to navigable waterways for trade with the First Nations peoples further inland; and it allowed for trade with peoples of the Low Arctic as they came south to gather wood for fuel and construction purposes. Beginning in 1717 and continuing well into the 1770s, the fort was transformed from wooden structures to a fortress built of limestone. To produce quicklime for the mortar used in the fort's construction, fuel was taken from the surrounding lands. This 18th-century harvest depressed the treeline several kilometres south of its original location, to which it still has not returned. These developments all took place during the Little Ice Age. Although the people were hardy it took them more than a century before the Hudson's Bay Company awoke from an institutional torpor on the shores of a frozen bay to expand their trading forts inland. Today, with a more benign climate, the area's transportation needs are served by an airport and a unique railway across tracks resting on what is essentially a bog,

from Gillam to Manitoba's only seaport, Churchill.

Churchill is also a tourist destination. Visitors can see polar bears roaming free in their native haunts close to the coast. The overly-adventurous can also experience the fear of being hunted when they disregard warnings about North America's largest terrestrial predator. Polar bears are cute but they also have to eat. The Arctic fox, wolf, lemmings, snowshoe hare, caribou herds, ptarmigan, raven, snow geese, and other waterfowl all make their appearance here. Some are permanent residents while others, such as caribou and snow geese, are migratory. Each of these species has developed special adaptations to survive these cold environments where conditions for plant growth are suitable for less than 100 days per year. As plant productivity is extremely low in this cold environment, animal populations are correspondingly low and sparse. It thus takes some doing to be lucky enough to encounter the denizens of this region.

ABOVE: *Failing light on tundra*
HUDSON BAY LOWLANDS NEAR CHURCHILL, MB

Spruce trees covered in snow
HUDSON BAY LOWLANDS NEAR CHURCHILL, MB

Spruce trees along the rocky shoreline of Hudson Bay
HUDSON BAY LOWLANDS NEAR CHURCHILL, MB

Female rock ptarmigan
HUDSON BAY LOWLANDS NEAR CHURCHILL, MB

Camouflaged Arctic hare behind a rock during a winter storm
HUDSON BAY LOWLANDS NEAR CHURCHILL, MB

Arctic fox leaping after prey
HUDSON BAY LOWLANDS NEAR CHURCHILL, MB

Polar bear walking across the frozen tundra during a winter storm
HUDSON BAY LOWLANDS NEAR CHURCHILL, MB

Polar bear sow and cubs resting in the shelter of willows
HUDSON BAY LOWLANDS NEAR CHURCHILL, MB

Polar bear waiting patiently
HUDSON BAY LOWLANDS NEAR CHURCHILL, MB

Two young male polar bears sparring on frozen tundra
Hudson Bay Lowlands near Churchill, MB

Arctic tern in flight
HUDSON BAY LOWLANDS NEAR CHURCHILL, MB

Inukshuk on rocky shoreline of Hudson Bay at Cape Merry
HUDSON BAY LOWLANDS NEAR CHURCHILL, MB

215

Lapland Rosebay (Rhododendron) carpeting the tundra in early summer
Hudson Bay Lowlands near Churchill, MB

TOP LEFT: *Semipalmated plover.* NEAR CHURCHILL, MB
TOP RIGHT: *Whimbrel.* NEAR CHURCHILL, MB
BOTTOM LEFT: *Willow ptarmigan.* NEAR CHURCHILL, MB
BOTTOM RIGHT: *American golden plover.* NEAR CHURCHILL, MB

Rocky shoreline along Hudson Bay
HUDSON BAY LOWLANDS NEAR CHURCHILL, MB

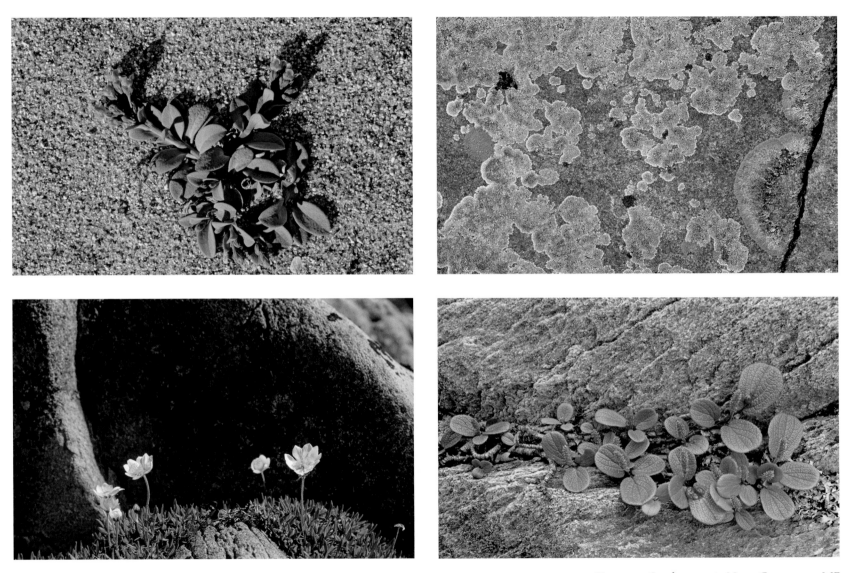

TOP LEFT: *Sea lungwort*. NEAR CHURCHILL, MB
TOP RIGHT: *Lichens on rock*. NEAR CHURCHILL, MB
BOTTOM LEFT: *White mountain avens*. NEAR CHURCHILL, MB
BOTTOM RIGHT: *Snow willow*. NEAR CHURCHILL, MB

219

Autumn-coloured vegetation along the sandy shoreline of Hudson Bay
Hudson Bay Lowlands near Churchill, MB

Large-flowered wintergreen blossom
HUDSON BAY LOWLANDS NEAR CHURCHILL, MB

Tree line and granite at sunset
HUDSON BAY LOWLANDS NEAR CHURCHILL, MB

Veins in rock
HUDSON BAY LOWLANDS NEAR CHURCHILL, MB

Precambrian rock along the Hudson Bay coastline
HUDSON BAY LOWLANDS NEAR CHURCHILL, MB

Detail of Precambrian rock at sunset
Hudson Bay Lowlands near Churchill, MB

Moon and rocks
Hudson Bay Lowlands near Churchill, MB

226

Intimate view of Precambrian rock
HUDSON BAY LOWLANDS NEAR CHURCHILL, MB

Sunrise over iceberg-covered Hudson Bay
HUDSON BAY LOWLANDS NEAR CHURCHILL, MB

Precambrian rock and ice along the Hudson Bay coastline
<small>HUDSON BAY LOWLANDS NEAR CHURCHILL, MB</small>

TOP LEFT: *Iceberg at sunrise.* NEAR CHURCHILL, MB
TOP RIGHT: *Icebergs on Hudson Bay.* NEAR CHURCHILL, MB
BOTTOM LEFT: *Stranded iceberg.* NEAR CHURCHILL, MB
BOTTOM RIGHT: *Iceberg at sunrise.* NEAR CHURCHILL, MB

Intimate view of ice in Hudson Bay in dawn light
HUDSON BAY LOWLANDS NEAR CHURCHILL, MB

231

Grain elevators and rail line in morning fog
Culross, MB

Mike Grandmaison's stories behind the photos

Front Cover: A Saskatchewan Wheat Pool grain elevator stands sentinel over a couple of old tractors and buildings. Bents, now a ghost town, was established around 1905, the time Saskatchewan and Alberta joined the Canadian Confederation.

p.i This is a place where you can experience what the prairies would have been like before they were settled some 200 years ago. You can imagine the bison roaming the grasslands and occasionally rubbing themselves against the large prairie stones.

p.vi John William Rayner came to Canada in 1903 and settled in Baljennie. He named the homestead Bolton Farm after his home in England. Today, Bill and Joan Rayner still farm this land. This story is probably echoed in many prairie families.

p.x Rainbows are fleeting, elusive, and short-lived. While chasing a storm down country roads with colleague Dave Reede, I managed to take a couple of images of this amazing rainbow, despite a clumsy fall which broke my glasses and nearly broke my neck. A polarizing filter enhances the colours.

pp.4-5 Southern Manitoba boasts the most colourful summer landscapes across the country with its amazing variety of crops that offer a visual feast for the eye.

Bold primary colours are emphasized through the use of a long telephoto lens to compress the perspective.

p.6 The Qu'Appelle Valley formed some 10,000 years ago, as the last continental ice sheet over Saskatchewan retreated and melted with the warming climate. Waters flowed eastwards across the ice sheet, scouring the land and creating a 180 m-deep, 2 km-wide valley.

p.7 The Qu'Appelle River flows 430 km eastwards from Lake Diefenbaker in southwestern Saskatchewan and joins the Assiniboine River in Manitoba just south of Lake of the Prairies.

p.8 Old wooden granaries like these are still found across the prairies, but like their taller siblings—the

grain elevators—they are also fast disappearing. Fair-weather cumulus clouds add to the romantic notion of the prairies.

p.9 Vintage Pioneer grain elevator make for bold and colourful abstract studies and are captured here with a long telephoto lens.

p.10 Today, canola is one of Canada's most valuable crops. Canola is often swathed and allowed to cure until the seed has ripened before it is picked up by a combine.

p.11 The Pembina Hills contain many high vantage points that offer views like this one. Panoramas of yellow canola fields stretching as far as the eye can see are more common today than they were in the past.

p.12 Parrish and Heimbecker is a private, family-owned Canadian business founded in 1909. At the height of the agricultural industry in 1935, about 5,700 prairie sentinels dotted the landscape, whereas now, fewer than 350 remain.

p.13 An old Vauxhall car sits abandoned in a field, along with an old church and two derelict grain elevators. During its heyday, the town had four grain elevators.

p.14 Wheat is grown in different parts of the country, but the greatest amount is found on the prairies. Wheat comes in two main categories: durum and non-durum. Non-durum wheat is used by either the milling industry to produce flour or by the livestock feed industry. Durum

wheat, on the other hand, is used to make pastas and semolina.

p.15 Canada is known worldwide for producing excellent quality durum wheat and is, in fact, the leading exporter of durum wheat in the world.

p.16 Sunflower production is relatively small in Canada and most of it occurs in Manitoba. Oilseed sunflowers are used in both birdfeed and the crushing industry for sunflower oil.

p.17 This bean field is the same field on which the sunflowers previously shown grew. From the top of this very hilly landscape, one can create interesting compositions using long telephoto lenses to extract intimate views from the greater landscape.

p.18 This is one of my favourite prairie images. In a minimalist way, it captures the drama of weather and colour in the open prairie and underlines the point that not every image needs a sunny blue sky!

p.19 The prairie skies are alive with bird life, from the great migrations of spring and fall to the quieter moments of a lazy summer afternoon.

p.20 Similarly, the ground is teeming with life, from the ubiquitous ground squirrel, to the cute "bunny" and chatty squirrel photos taken on my Winnipeg lawn. The black-tailed prairie dog, on the other hand, is now listed as a threatened species and is found in a very limited area of grasslands in southern Saskatchewan.

p.21 Red samphire often grows along the edges of alkali flats, shores, and ditches, appearing much like a red carpet. This plant removes excess salt by moving it to the tips of its stems, which then simply break off.

p.22 The three-flowered avens grows across the prairie provinces and provides small bees with an important source of food for insects emerging from hibernation.

p.23 As the flower develops and matures, the seed head resembles "Old Man's Whiskers" or "Prairie Smoke," the other names given to the plant. Early to mid-June weather offers carpets of this very attractive wildflower, which can be particularly beautiful when backlit by either a rising or a setting sun.

p.24 Before the arrival of the European settlers, the Red River Valley of southern Manitoba was covered by a vast sea of tall grass prairie. Today, the tall grass prairie in Manitoba represents a mere 1% of its former 6,000 km² range. Big bluestem grass or turkey foot is the characteristic species.

p.25 The prairie crocus, Manitoba's floral emblem, is one of the first prairie wildflowers to bloom in the spring. It is not uncommon to see this flower covered in snow at some point during its flowering stage as a result of a late spring snowfall.

p.26 Carpets of wildflowers like these asters are a sight to see in September.

p.27 Beef cattle production is highest in Alberta and the Hereford breed represents about 70% of Canadian herds. The prairies represent about 13% of the overall dairy production in Canada. Before cattle, however, pronghorns roamed the prairies, attaining speeds of up to 110 km/h.

p.28 Wild bergamot or bee balm is a common native wildflower that belongs to the mint family. Like other mints, it has medicinal purposes. Its leaves have been used in making herbal tea such as Earl Grey.

p.29 The three wildflowers depicted here can all be found in the tall grass prairie. Of these, the western prairie fringed orchid is a rare and threatened species that requires pollination from a hawk moth to survive.

p.30 Erosional forces have sculpted these sandstone outcrops found in the Souris Valley. The faces of many rocks are inscribed with carvings dating from pre-contact times to today's graffiti of initials. La Roche Percee Provincial Historic Site is a sacred First Nations site.

p.31 The word "coulee" comes from the French word "couler," which means "to flow." It generally refers to a gully or ravine that was shaped from erosional forces due to glacial activity.

p.32 The Conglomerate Cliffs are made of gravel and stone that have been cemented together by the calcium carbonate precipitated from water draining at the edge of the cliff. This conglomerate, overlooking Adam's Lake, protects the Cypress Hills from the

erosional forces of the wind and water.

p.33 The large reddish sandstone concretions or boulders found in this area have eroded from softer bedrock called the Bearspaw formation. These concretions are in various stages of breakdown and can measure up to 2.5 metres in diameter.

p.34 A long exposure of 30 seconds captured multiple lightning strikes during an extremely windy storm as the sun finally broke through to spill light over the landscape, creating a double rainbow. The driving rain made me shudder through the dozen or so attempts I made to take this photo, all while holding onto my tripod, which almost blew away.

p.35 A country back road leads through the farmland of a

northern Alberta town as the last light of a setting sun bathes the landscape with a warm glow.

p.36 The landscape around Maple Creek is one of high rolling hills that simply invite you to climb to the highest point and have a look. In this area I have often seen pronghorns racing across the prairie.

p.37 Abandoned farmhouses are plentiful on the prairie. I often like to include them as part of a landscape scene rather than making a portrait of them. They not only provide a focal point for my composition but also add a "human element."

p.38 The American bison once roamed the grasslands in the millions but by the late 1800s, few animals remained. Today they are relegated to small herds in a handful of protected

areas. Despite their massive size, they can move relatively fast, up to 55 km/h.

p.39 Morning is a magical time, mostly quiet with few people around. I composed this image by framing it between these two trees and waiting for the sun to eventually rise between them. In the summer, it is not unusual for me to get up at 3:00 a.m. so that I can get to a location in time to catch the sunrise.

p.40 A high vantage point allowed me to isolate a pattern in this winter scene where the snow barely covers the stubble field. Terrains of rolling hills are common in southwestern Alberta.

p.41 The last rays of the sun shine brightly on the cattail stems at the edge of the Seine River in Winnipeg. The warm, yellow colour of the vegetation contrasts sharply

with the cool, blue colour of the snow.

p.42 I love the landscape where the prairie meets the mountains, which occurs and is particularly beautiful in extreme southwestern Alberta. An approaching front will surely drop some moisture on the prairie.

p.43 Animals, whether wild or domestic, brave the elements at all times. Even though I know they are adapted to their environments, I can still feel the chill.

p.44 I enjoy the winter season. As a nature photographer, I am in a position to capture impressions of the natural world which few others ever experience. It is a quiet time that allows me to enjoy solitude and to appreciate the unique qualities of yet another part of the natural sequence of events in our northern climate.

p.45 Red barns are a favourite amongst photographers. The strong colour contrasts sharply against the bright snow and hoarfrost of winter. I wish that every farmer could paint their barns every few years, although other colours would be welcome, too.

p.46 Getting up early to photograph a sunrise is no guarantee that the sun will actually shine; but, if you don't get up, you most certainly won't capture the photograph.

p.47 This is one of the prettiest, if not the most colourful, little churches I have come across on the prairies. I haven't seen many red-coloured churches although I did come across two others when driving through Saskatchewan.

p.48 The town of Bents has been empty since the mid 1960s. This building served as a general store, a post office, and a private dwelling. I waited until dusk to "paint light" onto the building using a large flashlight during a 30-second exposure.

p.49 Excellent technique and a sturdy tripod are essential elements in capturing sharp images at such high magnification. I used the equivalent lens/camera combination of a 630-mm lens during a one-second exposure to capture a rising moon that also reflected brightly in a prairie slough.

p.50 Photography is essentially about light. Any scene, no matter how mundane it may look at a particular time, can be transformed by light! Dramatic light is

often fleeting and photographers go to great lengths to capture this elusive moment.

p.51 Sun dogs or parhelia are formed by refraction in hexagonal ice crystals. Two luminous spots appear on either side of the sun at about 22 degrees on both sides and at the same elevation as the sun.

p.52 Rarely have I encountered the following weather conditions at the same time in late fall: fog and frost with foliage in autumn colour. The willow tree begged to be exposed!

p.53 The prairie can be cold. With the wind blowing, it was bone-chilling on this particular morning even when the sun shone brightly. Dressing warmly in layers can make the difference between

being able to photograph in some sort of comfort or being simply too cold to produce anything worthwhile.

p.54 Writing-on-Stone Provincial Park is one of my favourite locations to photograph hoodoos. A hoodoo is a mushroom-shaped sandstone feature sculpted naturally by frost and driving rain. The hoodoo cap is made of harder rock that is resistant to weathering and thus protects the underlying, softer sandstone.

pp.58-59 The East Block of Grasslands National Park, also known as the Killdeer Badlands, differs from the softer, rolling terrain of the West Block. The badlands were formed by ancient glacial melt channels during the last Ice Age and the continued strong erosional forces of water and wind.

p.60 Castle Butte, made of sandstone and compressed clay, stands 70 m tall in the Big Muddy Badlands and can be seen protruding from the surrounding flat prairie from a long distance away. It is rumoured that the outlaw "The Sundance Kid" was once seen in the area.

p.61 Writing-on-Stone Provincial Park is one of the most important spiritual sites for the Blackfoot People. It also contains the largest concentration of rock art images on the Great Plains.

p.62 On a walk through the grasslands, one often encounters sandstone outcrops at the edge of the ravines that lead to badlands. Be wary of where you sit down, as cacti are common in the area. I can still find traces

of their spines from the last time I sat down!

p.63 The colour of the earth varies from place to place and can take on a very warm cast that is most visible at the beginning and end of the day. A long telephoto lens allowed me to capture a tight composition along the Little Bow River as the sun was dipping below the horizon.

p.64 The Milk River meanders through the badland terrain in Writing-on-Stone Provincial Park. During heavy rains, the white silt from the badlands is washed away into the river, imparting to it a "milky" look, and hence its name.

p.65 Walking amongst tall hoodoos can be quite an interesting experience, especially when one

unexpectedly encounters a deer on the trail. Be wary too when it's windy, as the blowing sandstone particles can create havoc with your equipment.

p.66 While we may all be familiar with the more popular badlands, many others remain to be discovered. A case in point are the badlands near Avonlea. The locals directed me to an area near town where a short walk across pastureland brought me to some badlands at the edge of the grasslands. They seemed to go on forever.

p.67 As I walk about the trails, I am always on the alert for surprise encounters with wildlife. While I would expect to see rattlesnakes in the badlands, I would not expect to see black bears and cougars; however, some folks warn that these larger animals are not uncommon in the area.

p.68 Dinosaur Provincial Park is Canada's largest badlands area and famous for being one of the richest dinosaur fossil areas in the world. It is also a UNESCO World Heritage Site.

p.69 This intimate view depicts small sandstone debris that has washed down from higher points during torrential rains that occur from time to time.

p.70 It is a relatively easy climb to the top of Castle Butte, but coming back down can be a different story. If hiking by yourself with a heavy pack, it may be difficult to negotiate the narrow passages in some places. I even had to throw down my camera pack at one point because the path was too narrow and steep for everything to fit through.

p.71 Situated along the Red Deer River, this park also features badland topography. It was named after a large plateau from which the Cree people once drove bison en masse off the cliffs in order to provide for their community.

p.72 I recently hiked a gruelling 15-20 km down into the Killdeer Badlands with some colleagues, walking from butte to butte. The dry, 30-plus-Celsius-degree weather was challenging but we prepared well by starting early in the day, bringing along an adequate supply of water and food, hats, and good walking boots.

p.73 The Sandcastle in the Beechy area along Diefenbaker Lake is not well-known. It is deceptively challenging to hike from the ...

cont'd p.236

upper grasslands to the bottom of the badlands. I often choose my 70-200 mm lens as my "go-to" lens to pull details and patterns from the greater landscape.

p.74 Hoodoos come in different shapes, sizes, and colours, depending on the erosional forces that have acted upon them as well as the geological formation from which they came.

p.75 The badlands of the Red Deer River valley near East Coulee are often referred to as the Drumheller Badlands. They are interesting to explore at different times, even in the middle of a winter storm.

p.76 After a rain, sandstone and clay can be quite slippery and caution should be exercised so as not to injure oneself. During the hour on

either side of sunrise and sunset, the quality of the sunlight imparts a beautiful warm cast on the badlands that can vary tremendously in colour even within the span of a few feet.

p.77 In the shade under sunny conditions, the light is remarkably cool; however, our eyes adjust so quickly that these differences may be imperceptible at the time. Film or digital can capture and record colours more truly.

p.78 I photographed for a few hours in the early afternoon and then decided to wait until later in the evening to catch the warm light on the dunes. However, clouds rolled in unexpectedly and put a damper on my plans. A few minutes before the sun dipped beneath the horizon, a break in the clouds allowed the sun to light up the scene brilliantly.

p.79 For the next few minutes I scurried about, trying to make as many different compositions as possible. At times like these, knowing your equipment and techniques well can really pay off. I woke up the next morning to heavy, overcast skies.

p.80 While most arid areas in Canada may not technically be deserts, they are nonetheless very dry lands that often feature large tracts of sandy areas or dunes. Because landmarks are difficult to see or nonexistent in some areas, one can easily get lost.

p.81 Front light, sidelight or backlight can impart a very different look on a particular dune, depending on the angle of the sun on a particular dune. In this image, sidelight creates interesting textures and patterns in the sand.

p.82 The Carberry (Spirit Sands) Desert features stabilized dunes from grasses, shrubs, and trees, as well as open sandy areas. It also covers an extensive area that far exceeds what you see from the trail.

p.83 In very dry areas like the Carberry Desert, one tends to find unique plants such as prairie sunflowers, prickly pear, and pincushion cacti, and animals such as the hognose snake and the prairie skink.

p.84 The Great Sand Hills consist of at least a couple of dozen dune sections ranging in height from 15 to 35 m. The dunes are located here and there on the native prairie that surrounds them. On occasion, one may encounter cattle, but one is far more likely to see mule deer.

p.85 When I hike into dune habitat, I often wrap my camera and lens in a plastic bag when the wind blows sand around. Once I have decided upon a composition, I remove the camera from the plastic, make a few quick exposures, and return it to the plastic bag.

p.86 A few grains of sand can easily jam a lens or work their way into the camera's interior. Before a hike, I will often decide which lens I might want to use and attach one each to two different bodies in order to avoid changing lenses when it's windy.

p.87 I'm always looking for small, interesting details to add variety to a portfolio such as these tiny "sand hoodoos," vegetation, or patterns in the sand.

p.88 The shorter days of autumn trigger the process of leaves changing colour. As trees begin to shut down for the winter, the green chlorophyll pigment slowly disappears from the leaves. Other pigments, which have been present all along, begin to predominate and impart different colours to the leaves.

pp.92-93 Climbing a hillside to gain a higher vantage point often helps me to isolate a nice grouping of colour. The yellow creates a pleasing pattern with the alternating green of the trees whose foliage has not yet changed colour. The dark green conifers offer additional colour contrast.

p.94 Trembling aspen or white poplar trees are hardwoods or deciduous trees, which means they lose their leaves in

the fall. Evergreens or coniferous trees, on the other hand, do not shed their needles (leaves) and remain foliated throughout the season.

p.95 Autumn colours are at their brightest in late summer when the weather is dry, and in autumn when the days are sunny and the evenings are cool and crisp, but not freezing. A warm period in the fall can significantly lessen the colour intensity.

p.96 The eastern larch tree is a conifer (cone bearing tree) that sheds its needles (leaves) in the fall after turning a bright yellow-orange colour.

p.97 Trees beautify our surroundings, purify our air, act as sound barriers, and manufacture precious oxygen. They affect our climate by moderating the effects of the sun, wind, and

rain. Trees act as a carbon sink by removing carbon dioxide from the air and storing it as cellulose in their trunks, branches, and roots. They also provide shelter for wildlife.

p.98 Urban forests like the Bois-des-esprits located along the Seine River in Winnipeg are important not only for providing green spaces in an otherwise concrete environment but also for providing corridors around watercourses.

p.99 Many types of plants can be found under a canopy of trees—everything from clubmosses, to mushrooms, to wildflowers. As they die, they decompose and provide nutrients for other living organisms.

p.100 Fogbows form when cloud droplets are so small that

bands of colour begin to overlap and mix, producing a white bow with only the slightest hint of yellow on the outside. They are also known as cloudbows, mistbows or white rainbows.

p.101 A rainbow is always found in the opposite direction of the sun. At sunrise or sunset, when the sun is on the horizon, a rainbow is a full half-circle high and at its highest possible height. Polarizing filters enhance the intensity of a rainbow's colour but care must be exercised so as not to completely eliminate the colour!

p.102 Trees have been a major focal point throughout my career. I worked in forestry for close to 18 years and then spent the remainder of my working career as a nature photographer.

p.103 Waking up before sunrise is not easy, nor is it my favourite thing to do. Depending on how far my destination might be, I might be awake at 3:30 a.m. in order to arrive well ahead of a 5:30 a.m. sunrise! Here I captured a composition of tree trunks bathed by the warm, foggy light of sunrise.

p.104 "Never place your subject (or horizon) in the middle of the photograph" is a commonly known rule of composition. Doing so tends to produces a more static scene, which is precisely the effect I wanted to emphasize for this serene and peaceful mood.

p.105 Dramatic light is often fleeting. Frequently we need to react quickly and make choices about where to point the lens. In forests, the light can vanish even before you get the

chance to press the shutter. I managed only a couple of exposures before the sun disappeared.

p.106 While I can appreciate the difficulty in obtaining a portrait of an animal, I prefer photographing an animal as a part of its environment. This owl moved from tree to tree a few times before finally settling in and allowing me to photograph it for as long as I wanted.

p.107 Lichens are important colonizers of barren ground and rock. Because they are very sensitive to changes in the environment, they are also excellent ecological indicators of pollution.

p.108 A light rain doesn't necessarily deter me from photographing. At such times, colours become more saturated, as can be seen in the brightly coloured

bark of these young aspens. I delight in trying to organize order from chaos.

p.109 Black spruce trees are an important component of our boreal forests, the second-largest biome on Earth. Needles and cones of coniferous trees such as black spruce are an important source of food for birds like the spruce grouse, particularly in winter.

p.110 Fire is a natural and important part of the functioning of numerous forest ecosystems. A few days following a major fire, I walked into this jack pine forest to record the devastation. It was an eerie experience, particularly when the occasional wind would blow the ashes around, causing a light dust cloud on the forest floor.

p.111 A light coating of frost blankets the

colourful pine forest floor. It won't be long now before snow settles in.

p.112 Understanding the natural history of a species is vital to knowing when and where to find it. These orchids are three out of about 25 species that I have photographed in this region.

p.113 Black spruce grows on a variety of sites but is often found on poorly drained sites, sometimes associated with larch (tamarack). Black spruce has been an important tree species for Canada, particularly in its use as pulpwood in the production of paper. Because of its long, strong fibres, it produces very high-quality pulp.

p.114 I enjoy working with a short-to-medium telephoto

lens to create intimate views. I isolated a couple of colourful dogwood twigs against a background pattern of lichen on rock.

p.115 I used the same lens as in the image opposite to compose this image of dogwood berries in the fall. I'm always amazed at the kaleidoscope of colour found in the underbrush.

p.116 I was photographing a stormy scene on a lake when I turned around and noticed a bright rainbow down the road. I quickly jumped into my vehicle and drove a kilometre to find an interesting composition. While no more than a couple of minutes had elapsed, much of the rainbow had vanished.

p.117 Dressing appropriately is the key

to enjoying the great outdoors in all seasons. The most challenging aspect of winter photography for me is overcoming the psychological barrier of leaving my warm, cozy, comfortable bed to go outside in the cold to photograph a sunrise.

p.118 I walked along this short boardwalk creating various compositions for about three hours before I realized that I had frostbite on my nose. It was all worth it.

p.119 The blue colour of the surface snow is a result of the blue sky reflected by the snow. There are actually tree saplings underneath these mounds of snow.

p.120 In winter, the snow that blankets the ground simplifies compositions by covering up much of the debris found on the

forest floor during other seasons.

p.121 I slip on a pair of snowshoes to help me get around outdoors when the snow is deep, especially after a heavy snowfall. Thick hoarfrost like this creates a veritable winter wonderland—"picture-perfect," one might even say.

p.122 After a snowstorm, I'm usually quite excited about exploring the outdoors to capture the aftermath of the storm before the winds begin to blow and the sun melts the freshly fallen snow.

p.123 A local urban park can provide plenty of interesting photographic opportunities and allows me time to discover compositions without requiring me to venture miles away.

p.124 A jack pine forest provides a nice foreground to a backdrop of stars trailing during a 45-minute-long exposure. The greenish colour in the sky is the result of low-level northern light activity that was barely noticeable to the eye.

p.125 When northern light activity seems promising, I often scout ahead of time locations that have good foreground possibilities. I have a favourite location near my home to which I can drive rather quickly if necessary. Exposures between ten and ninety seconds are required depending on the intensity of the light.

p.126 Dawn brings promise of a memorable day to come. The judicious use of neutral graduated filters coupled with HDR (high dynamic range) technique produced a breathtaking view of this wetland.

pp.130-131 Water provides Earth with the capacity to support life. It covers 70% of the earth's surface, of which only 2.5% is freshwater. As I travel across the country, I notice people have their favourite location to watch the sun set.

p.132 As more people migrate to cities, fewer people experience the natural environment. As a species, we are less and less connected to the natural world—our land, our skies, our water, our forests, and our creatures.

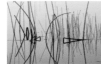

p.133 Our existence on this earth represents but a fraction of the earth's existence. Yet, we make decisions daily that are threatening the planet's health and even its very survival. Our welfare and that of all the other species depends upon a healthy planet which we have taken for granted for far too long.

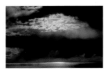

p.134 I have seen many storms develop over Lesser Slave Lake over the years. Exposing for the highlights retains important detail which enhances the drama of the scene.

p.135 "Lining up my ducks": I watched closely from the corner of my eye as the ducks swam by one by one and climbed onto the rock. A split-second decision to click the shutter caught them just before they were back in the water.

p.136 Wetlands are the primary habitat of many animal species. Wetlands are ecologically important because they remove and store greenhouse gases from the Earth's atmosphere, slowing the effects of global warming.

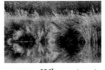

p.137 What is in front of the lens says as much about the person making the image as it says about the subject matter itself. I love the asymmetrical reflection in this image.

p.138 Frost arrives and some autumn colour hangs on, a signal that winter is not far behind. It's almost a season unto itself, the one between fall and winter.

p.139 In this contemplative scene, the stillness of the air creates a colourful, mirror-like reflection of the shoreline trees that is almost mesmerizing.

p.140 Morning is my favourite time of day for photography. It tends to be peaceful, to have little sense of urgency, and offers plenty of time to absorb the moment.

p.141 Prairie potholes are depressions left by glacier recession during the last ice age. Along with rivers, lakes, ponds, and oceans, they provide habitat for all sorts of wildlife, including birds.

p.142 "Serendipity," "happy accident"—and "pleasant surprise" could all describe this situation. I was photographing this lily blossom when I ran out of space on my memory card. After running to get another card, I returned and looked into the viewfinder only to discover that a leopard frog had comfortably settled in!

p.143 A polarizing filter reduces glare from foliage, helps to penetrate through water, and increases contrast between elements. It works by aligning the scattered wavelengths of light into one direction, thus deepening the colour.

p.144 What a night this was! For half an hour, I scrambled to make as many different compositions as possible, aware that the northern lights display might only last seconds. I have also spent hours and even entire nights waiting for something to happen. Patience is definitely a virtue worth learning.

p.145 This tapestry of yellow water lilies was captured with a long lens and maximum depth of field in order to render all the lily pads sharp, from edge to edge. I am always searching for intimate and unusual compositions which I find to be more personal and characteristic of vision and style.

p.146 Consider tilting the camera to a vertical position to make a portrait of your subject, to increase the sense of depth and space in an image or simply because it works well with the elements of the composition.

p.147 Dorothea Lange once said: "The camera is an instrument that teaches people how to see without a camera." I have found this to be so true.

p.148 I'm a big fan of photographing clouds and I am always aware of how clouds affect the composition in a landscape. I take care to create an interesting balance between clouds and other elements in my photographs and ensure the clouds do not appear haphazardly in the frame.

p.149 This classic, "silky" look of falling water was captured using a slow shutter speed on my tripod-mounted camera. To obtain long exposures on a bright day, reduce the amount of light reaching the sensor by inserting a neutral density or a polarizing filter in front of the lens.

p.150 In this digital era, professional quality images are best produced in RAW format. Unlike the "jpg format," RAW, if properly exposed, captures all available digital information with few compromises. Back in the studio, photographers process RAW files in order to bring out the subtleties of a particular scene.

p.151 In addition to being a skilled craftsman with

an excellent sense of design, today's professional photographer must also be a competent image processor. Like many other art forms, photography has also evolved. Few of the labs that once processed all our film remain.

p.152 I can easily lose myself for hours creating abstract images of water. Long lenses are ideal for extracting or selecting details. Much of the time is spent looking.

p.153 Water levels may fluctuate greatly both seasonally and depending on the amount of moisture that falls in a particular year. To capture the swirling motion of water during a bright, sunny day, I used a variable neutral density filter which lengthened the exposure to eight seconds.

p.154 One must be alert to notice and capture unusual lighting conditions.

p.155 Little Limestone Lake is the world's largest marl lake and was recently protected under the creation of Little Limestone Lake Provincial Park. Marl is created when calcite from the local limestone is precipitated from warm water. As the temperature rises, so does the quantity of marl, which changes the colour of the lake.

p156 The iconic wooden stilt piers on the west side of Lake Winnipeg are most often built from local aspen trees. These unique structures are rebuilt every spring because the powerful ice that forms on the lake would otherwise destroy them.

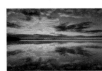

p.157 This tranquil, early morning cloud reflection is an excellent example of formal, symmetrical balance, creating a mirror image of the horizon.

p.158 The first couple of hours around sunrise and sunset are often a photographer's favourite time to photograph landscapes, as the sunlight at this time is particularly warm in colour.

p.159 The eastern shore of Lake Manitoba near Steep Rock features tall limestone cliffs that are a delight to explore. Walking along the shoreline reveals captivating views, including small underwater caves.

p.160 I love the contrast of cool and

warm colours. For this image, I abstracted the bands of colour at dusk using a moderate telephoto lens. "Anyone who keeps the ability to see beauty never grows old," said Franz Kafka. I hope he's right!

p.161 The beauty of this scene betrays the frigid conditions it was photographed under. Temperatures hovered around -40 degrees Celsius with a strong wind to boot. I could barely compose and click the shutter before needing to turn away for a few minutes. I have never been so cold!

p.162 In the spring, the ice breaks up from the heat and wind action. It gets pushed around and often ends up on the shore, creating glorious opportunities for photographing against the light.

p.163 Texture is the surface quality of things and is enhanced by the low, warm light illuminating this scene from the top left corner of the image. The ice had broken up the day before but refroze overnight, which resulted in an interesting pattern of shapes and colour.

p.164 It was a glorious morning; the air was cool, the water calm, and the fog thick. I waited for the sunlight to rise above the eastern mountains and finally illuminate the peak of Pyramid Mountain. A couple of neutral graduated filters held in front of a wide-angle lens retained a range of exposure in this high-contrast scene.

p.168 Photography is a waiting game. I waited for more than an hour on the shore of Medicine Lake for

any kind of light to break through the clouds. Nothing happened, so I left. Five minutes later the sun finally peeked through, so I stopped and captured the Colin Range in failing light.

p.169 This park is well out of the way. If you are looking for peace and quiet and exceptional scenery away from the crowds, look no further.

p.170 I captured first light on the peaks at Edith Cavell while the rest of the glacial lake and icebergs remained in shadow.

p.171 Herbert Lake is one of the gems of the Canadian Rockies. I arrived early and waited for Mother Nature to do her magic and she did!

p.172 Fog is essentially a cloud that comes in contact with the ground. On this particular occasion, the sun barely poked through except once and just enough to create a stunning contrast in colour.

p.173 Mountain weather is notoriously unpredictable. I have been skunked at Vermilion Lakes many times but I have captured a number of amazing scenes here, too. It's important to react quickly because the light may well disappear without notice.

p.174 Pyramid Mountain is named for the shape of its peak. It is the highest peak in the vicinity of Jasper townsite. I framed the scene with the waterlogged tree and rocky shore in the foreground to lure the viewer into the composition.

p.175 I was driving near Bow Summit as the sun was about to sink below the horizon. I looked frantically for a good foreground to make an image when I came upon this wetland. A very wide-angle lens allowed me to capture a broader view with plenty of detail in the foreground.

p. 176 You can access Leech Lake via the old Jasper Highway that runs by the Athabasca Falls. Peace and tranquility always seem to invite symmetry.

p.177 Some call Peyto Lake the most beautiful lake in the world. The truth is that a number of other lakes also qualify, such as Moraine Lake and Lake Louise. The turquoise of the lake comes from finely ground glacial flour or silt that flows into Peyto Lake from Peyto Glacier and the Wapta Icefield.

p.178 The Valley of the Ten Peaks includes Moraine Lake which was featured on the reverse side of the 1969 and the 1979 issues of the Canadian twenty-dollar bill. The scene is stunning at any time and it is no wonder it is usually crowded here.

p.179 Lake Louise is known to the Stoney Nakoda First Nations people as "Lake of the Little Fishes." It was named Lake Louise in 1884 in honour of Princess Louise Caroline Alberta, daughter of Queen Victoria. I've come here many times and I always enjoy its beauty.

p.180 Bow Lake is one in a series of lakes that lines the Icefields Parkway, the mountain highway that joins Banff to Jasper. I never tire of admiring the view.

p.181 Horseshoe Lake near Jasper is seldom crowded. On a calm day, the rocky shoreline at the south end of the lake offers endless possibilities to create images of reflections, unless of course someone dives from the nearby cliff and disturbs the water.

p.182 Castle Mountain in the background stands tall as fireweed grows along the meandering Bow River. The name was changed to Mount Eisenhower following a visit by the then president of the United States; however, public pressure forced the name to change back to Castle Mountain in 1979.

p.183 Elk are also called wapiti, which means "white rump." Like all wild animals, they should never be approached and can be particularly

dangerous during the rutting season in the fall.

p.184 The Maligne River cuts through 50-metre-high limestone walls of Maligne Canyon, one of the spectacular gorges of the Canadian Rockies. It plunges here over a scenic waterfall.

p.185 This is a detail of Cameron Falls located in the townsite of Waterton Village. It is the site of the oldest rock in the Canadian Rocky Mountain range. The Precambrian bedrock dates back some 1.5 billion years.

p.186 The David Thompson Highway runs from Red Deer to Saskatchewan Crossing in Banff National Park. Along the highway and closer to the park are many locations in which the aspen trees

turn from orange to red in the fall, as opposed to the more typical shift in colour from yellow to yellowish-orange.

p.187 A grouping of roadside aspens has partly turned colour.

p.188 Sunlight breaks through the heavy clouds and turns an otherwise lacklustre scene into a dramatic vista.

p.189 The alpine turns a multitude of colours in the fall.

p.190 Western larches turn orange-yellow in the fall. I like the contrast in texture from the smooth, colourful, organic larch trees compared to the rough, dull-grey, inorganic mountain peak.

p.191 Mountains provide an important habitat for many species. I marvel at the agility of the mountain goats and sheep as much as the power of bears. I am always amazed at how cavalier some tourists can be about their safety when they come close to bears.

p.192 Inclement weather offers different opportunities. The fog and low-cloud ceiling bring a moody, quiet feeling to this scene of the Bow River leaving Bow Falls.

p.193 A long lens has pulled in a section of a mountain engulfed by clouds, imparting to the scene the look of an etching.

p.194 The two images that make up this page spread were

made using long telephoto lenses to focus in on just a section of the mountain.

p.195 The Canadian Rockies get their name from the obvious massive composition of rocks that are mainly shale and limestone.

pp.196-197 I watched a cow moose and her calf walk along the sandbars of Medicine Lake for quite some time, so much so that I missed a sunset a few kilometres away that I had planned to photograph.

p.198 Warm light from a setting sun bathes a snow-covered landscape of stunted spruce. In winter, sunlight remains warm for an extended period of time.

pp.202-203 First light spills over

the Hudson Bay Lowlands. The wind is blowing, adding to the already cold frigid morning.

p.204 We stopped a tundra buggy long enough for me to capture an image of scattered spruce trees on the tundra with the blue of the earth's shadow showing above the horizon. The Belt of Venus is the pink band separating the Earth's shadow from the sky above.

p.205 Small spruce trees are nearly engulfed in snow, which provides important cover during the extreme cold of winter at this latitude.

p.206 The lack of detail in the snowy landscape from overcast conditions creates an etching-like image.

p.207 Ptarmigans are mostly found on the tundra and spend most of their lives on the ground. They have feathered feet, which help them walk on the snow and forage for plants.

p.208 With its thick white winter coat the Arctic hare is a master of camouflage, hiding in a snowdrift behind a rock. I had also made some portraits of the hare with a very long, 500-mm lens; however, for this image I switched to a camera equipped with a shorter (equivalent to 70 mm) lens to depict the animal in its environment.

p.209 Having seen this type of behaviour in red foxes further south, I anticipated that this fox might decide to leap after prey. Reacting quickly, I captured a series of images of the fox jumping deeper and deeper into the snow until only the tip of its tail showed.

p.210 I captured this quintessential northern scene, complete with a polar bear walking on the frozen tundra, during a winter storm. I liked the "white-on-white" colour palette that this scene presented.

p.211 A polar bear sow rests with her two cubs snuggled closely in the shelter of some shrubbery as the sun casts its last rays on the landscape. Churchill is considered the polar bear capital of the world.

p.212 "Nanuk" is the Inuit name for polar bear, the world's largest land carnivore. It is largely restricted to the Arctic Circle, although its range does descend further south into some areas like Churchill. Polar bears feed primarily on ringed and bearded seals that are hunted on the ice.

p.213 Two young male polar bears display sparring behaviour. Play fighting is their way of developing survival skills. They await the freezing of Hudson Bay so that they can once again return to the sea ice to feed. Canada is home to two thirds of the world's polar bear population. The bears are considered 'a species of special concern.'

p.214 The Arctic tern is a migratory seabird that breeds in the far north. It is recognized as having one of the longest migration routes in the world. It is known for exhibiting aggressive behaviour called "dive-bombing" if approached, particularly when a nest is nearby.

p.215 Cape Merry is a national historic site which affords a beautiful view of the mouth of the Churchill River and an excellent vantage point from which to watch beluga whales. This inukshuk was made years ago and is no longer standing. Inuksuit were historically erected by the Inuit as landmarks for travel and herding caribou.

p.216 Lapland rosebay is a low-growing, mat-forming evergreen shrub that grows on the subarctic tundra. Manitoba's only native rhododendron, the Lapland rosebay carpets large areas of the tundra with its colourful pink flowers in the early summer. The mountain avens similarly covers the tundra with its white flowers at the same time or shortly after.

p.217 Churchill is world famous for birdwatching. Early to mid-June is a great time to see northern migrants as well as local breeders in action, while late June is an excellent time to observe "on-the-nest" birds.

p.218 Outcrops of Precambrian Shield rocks form the western boundary of the Churchill area near its mouth as well as along the vicinity of the townsite. The rocks afford shelter to many plants as well as a substrate for lichens, a plant that is composed of algae and fungi living together in a mutually beneficial (symbiotic) relationship.

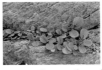

p.219 The tundra of the Hudson Bay Lowlands is far from being a barren wasteland. It supports a surprising variety of plants that have adapted to the severe environmental conditions.

p.220 Each habitat supports a specific association of plants called a plant community. This coastal zone habitat has sand as a substrate and is flooded regularly by salt water. Not suprisingly, this habitat supports plants that are tolerant of salt water.

p.221 The large-flowered wintergreen contains a drug related to aspirin. As I was reading about this species in Karen Johnson's Wildflowers of Churchill and the Hudson Bay Region, I noticed a few mosquitoes pressed between the pages—a testament to the abundance of these critters in the area!

p.222 I am particularly attracted by the rock in this area, from the small pebbles to the large outcrops, especially when the rock is bathed in warm light.

p.223 Here is a detail of a rock of different constituents, covered by orange-coloured lichen. I enjoy making abstract images like this one.

p.224 Heath plants line the edge of this grouping of rock at sunrise.

p.225 This detail of a rock was made with a small telephoto lens. When doing close-up photographs, it is important to ensure that every corner of the image is tack sharp. A small lens aperture, along with a sturdy tripod, go a long way toward creating crisp, sharp images.

p.226 The moon was captured above sun-washed rocks using a wide-angle lens. One must be vigilant on the Hudson Bay Lowlands about potential encounters with polar bears. They can easily be lurking behind a rock.

p.227 This image features another abstract closeup of rock. I first experienced the Low Arctic environment in the early 1970s as a summer student while assisting a master's student from McMaster University.

p.228 Hudson Bay is an immense inland sea that is almost entirely surrounded by land. It is connected to both the Arctic and Atlantic Oceans. This image was made at sunrise around Canada Day.

p.229 The climate along Hudson Bay can vary dramatically even in a matter of hours. I remember that on one particular day the temperatures hovered in the high 20 degrees Celsius only to plummet over the next three to four hours to just a few degrees above zero.

p.230 Climate change is certainly noticeable in the north. In the mid 1990s, I spent time on the coast photographing ice floes. Peak time for the best ice coming on shore was normally the last week in June or the first week in July. Fifteen years later, the ice in the area has often already disappeared by mid June.

p.231 I have always loved the quote by Leonardo da Vinci stating that "Simplicity is the ultimate sophistication." I composed this image of ice floes at dawn in such a way as to highlight the contrast of warm and cool colours.

p.232 The railway was an important tool in developing the West by transporting goods across the country. Grain elevators were strategically placed along railway lines to facilitate the distribution of grain. An early morning fog enhances the mood captured of this old Paterson Grain elevator.

Acknowledgements

Prairie and Beyond is the culmination of more than thirty years of exploring and photographing this wonderful region of Canada. A project of this magnitude involves many people who have given freely of their time, assistance, and support. I cannot mention them all, since I would surely miss some, but I do need to express my sincerest thanks to at least a few.

I am forever grateful to my friends and colleagues for providing advice, encouragement, companionship, and shelter:

Daryl Benson, Peter Blahut, Ian Bowden and Jean Tait, John and Cindy Bykerk, Carmain Chimko, Mike Egglestone, Dennis and Frieda Fast, Benoit Gauthier and Diane Lavoie, Carl Hanninen, Chris Insull, Don Johnston, Mike Karakas and Tami Reynolds, Reg and Evelyn Keele, Joe Kerr, Marilyn Latta and Bill Bremner, John Marriott, Paul and Shirley Martens, Mufty and Bill Mathewson, my colleagues at the Northern Forestry Centre, Rob Peters and Ev Richter, Roy Ramsay, Dave and Yvette Reede, Brad Smith, Bev and Doug Stich, Anil Sud, Andrew Toews, Dick Toews, Pat and Jan Volney, Ian Ward and Donna Danyluk, Darwin Wiggett;

Anil Sud for your "critical eye" throughout the editing and selecting of images;

Marilyn Latta, Dennis Fast, Ken Mallett, Ian Ward and Donna Danyluk for your able assistance in identifying plant and animal species;

Don Johnston for the portrait of yours truly on the cover flap;

Joan and Bill Rayner for your hospitality, for taking me around the countryside and filling me in on the history of the Rayner family and Bolton Farm;

Friesens Corporation, in particular Ray Friesen, Donovan Bergman, Fred Perrin, Jef Burnard, and all the support staff, including the pressmen, for your dedication to, enthusiasm for, and professionalism in helping me create yet another fine-looking book;

Jan Volney, my former supervisor in the Canadian Forest Service, for your friendship, your sense of fairness, your integrity, your respect and support over the years, and for your eloquent contribution to *Prairie and Beyond*;

my publisher, Turnstone Press—Jamis Paulson, Sharon Caseburg, Christine Mazur, and Sara Harms, along with Jen Magura—first for the opportunity to make this project happen, second for the freedom to create a work that is true to my vision, and finally for all your support and expertise in helping bring this project together with a smile;

and last but not least, my family—Annette, Vanessa, Nadine, Colin, Riley, and Barry for your support and love!

Un grand merci à tous!

—Mike Grandmaison